CU00484804

LEAVING THE ARENA

LEAVING THE ARENA

A Story of Bar and Bench

DAVID KEENE

BLOOMSBURY ACADEMIC
LONDON • NEW YORK • OXFORD • NEW DELHI • SYDNEY

BLOOMSBURY ACADEMIC
Bloomsbury Publishing Plc
50 Bedford Square, London, WC1B 3DP, UK
1385 Broadway, New York, NY 10018, USA

BLOOMSBURY, BLOOMSBURY ACADEMIC and the Diana logo are
trademarks of Bloomsbury Publishing Plc

First published in Great Britain 2020
Reprinted 2020

A catalogue record for this book is available from the British Library.

A catalog record for this book is available from the Library of Congress.

ISBN: 978-1-7883-1826-6
ePDF: 978-1-7867-3667-3
eBook: 978-1-7867-2661-2

Typeset by RefineCatch Limited, Bungay, Suffolk
Printed and bound in Great Britain

To find out more about our authors and books visit www.bloomsbury.com
and sign up for our newsletters.

For my wonderful granddaughters

Olivia
Rosalind
Lily
Violet
Flo

It is not the critic who counts;
not the man who points out how the strong man stumbles,
or where the doer of deeds could have done them better.
The credit belongs to the man who is actually in the arena,
whose face is marred by dust and sweat and blood;
who strives valiantly; who errs,
who comes short again and again,
because there is no effort without error and shortcoming;
but who does actually strive to do the deeds;
who knows great enthusiasms, the great devotions;
who spends himself in a worthy cause;
who at the best knows in the end the triumph of high
   achievement,
and who at the worst, if he fails,
at least fails while daring greatly,
so that his place shall never be with those cold and timid souls
   who neither know victory nor defeat.

Former President THEODORE ROOSEVELT,
The Sorbonne, Paris
23 April 1910

A judge who himself conducts the examination [of a witness]
descends into the arena and is liable to have his vision clouded
by the dust of the conflict.

LORD GREENE, M.R., in *Yuill v. Yuill*, 1945 P.15

CONTENTS

ILLUSTRATIONS

1. Mother, brother Andrew (on chair) and me.
2. Father.
3. On holiday in Dovercourt, about 1947.
4. G. J. N. Whitfield, Headmaster of Hampton Grammar School.
5. Balliol College, Oxford.
6. First fee note as barrister, 1965.
7. October 1974 election leaflet.
8. October 1974 election leaflet.
9. Early family life, with Harriet and Edward.
10. Gillian, Call to the Bar 1980. © Universal Pictorial Press and Agency Ltd.
11. Mother and father in retirement.
12. The site of South Woodham Ferrers town.
13. London City Airport. [copyright details tbc]
14. Matrix for High Court judges' robes for each occasion.
15. Macdonald libel case. [copyright details tbc]
16. The house at St Martin d'Oydes, France.
17. The village of St Martin d'Oydes (house in centre foreground).

ACKNOWLEDGEMENTS

A short autobiographical work like this has not involved many others – no researchers, no colleagues in specialist areas. Nonetheless, there are three people to whom I want to express my gratitude for their help in various ways.

The first is Lester Crook of the publishers I. B. Tauris & Co. Ltd. Lester has been a source of encouragement and support from the moment he received the first draft from me, a person he had never met or known. The second is Ann Kavanagh of my chambers, 39 Essex Chambers of Chancery Lane. With great apparent willingness, Ann agreed to turn my handwritten manuscript into a legible typed text and she put up, without complaint, being landed subsequently with a seemingly endless stream of additions and corrections.

Finally and above all, I would like to pay tribute to my wife, Gillian. This is not just because of the usual point made by authors about their spouse or partner having borne the burden of them disappearing for hours on end to write – though that is part of the contribution she has made. It goes beyond that, and it has taken a more positive form. Gillian's recollection of events during our fifty-plus years together has often been far more detailed and vivid than mine. In addition, she has retained information about my family and my life before she and I met, information gleaned from conversations with my parents and others. My gratitude to her is immense.

It goes without saying that any inaccuracies in this volume, and any offence any of it may cause, are my responsibility and mine alone.

David Keene

Oxford and London

FOREWORD

By Lord Woolf

I am most grateful to Sir David Keene for asking me to contribute this foreword. The motive of David for writing *Leaving the Arena* was for his 'wonderful' granddaughters, Olivia, Rosalind, Lily, Violet and Flo. He thought they would like to know more about his life. I am confident they will find the contents absorbing. I have also found this to be the case and it is because *Leaving the Arena* is such a 'good read' that I feel privileged to write this foreword. This is especially the case for me because although I am almost a decade older than David, he and I had very similar careers.

During the intervening decade, the justice system had not significantly changed, and neither David nor I had immediate families who had made the law their career. There were differences in our education but we both entered the profession as members of the Inner Temple. Neither he nor I had predetermined plans for our careers after we started practice. The areas in which we subsequently practised differed, but this was largely because of the chambers of which we were members. We were both able to promote our practice in areas where there was significant demand for the services of the Bar. In David's case, his practice developed because of the substantial planning inquiries which accompanied the creation of the new roads, airports and railways that were a requirement of post-war Britain. In those days success at the Bar led almost inevitably to an advocate becoming QC, leading counsel, and in due course David followed this course. He also became a part-time judge or Recorder and then at a relatively early age he became a member of the High Court Bench and the nature of his work changed significantly. For a time it was almost exclusively presiding over criminal trials with juries. Again, following the pattern of the times, he earned promotion to the Court of Appeal. This involved his administering justice not as a judge sitting alone but as part of a team of three Lord Justices of Appeal.

This was a hardworking but a fascinating and absorbing life. It was very much the same life as able lawyers had enjoyed for generations. Towards the end of David's career significant changes took place but their impact on senior judges were limited and the fascination of David's account of his career is that it is an admirable record of the traditional life of a barrister and a judge which is in the process of fundamental change so that in future those who follow in David's footsteps will have a very different career from that which David experienced.

The extent of the changes which are taking place mean that *Leaving the Arena* will be a record of a professional career which is now no more. But it is still highly relevant because it reflects the values of justice in this country which we need to preserve if we are to retain our reputation as a nation committed to the rule of law.

The significance of this is that not only in this country but also in other parts of the globe which hitherto had very different systems of justice from our own, there is an ambition to provide for their citizens qualities of justice which in this country are taken for granted but elsewhere are not available. So when David retired from the Bench in this country, he and I were engaged in promoting the virtues of an independent and incorrupt legal system in differing parts of the world.

David's description of the part that he played in this area, particularly on behalf of the Slynn Foundation and in Qatar, will be a further valuable bequest of *Leaving the Arena*.

Fortunately, David's succinct and attractive style of writing means that it is a pleasure for the reader to accompany him on his journey through the legal world. I very much hope that the journey is now by no means finished and in due course a supplement will be necessary. However, he can be proud of what he has achieved so far which is a remarkable record of the standards of our justice system to date.

IN THE ARENA

1

In the Beginning

Youth would be an ideal state if it came a little later in life.
HERBERT ASQUITH

I always say that there is nothing like a bout of atrial fibrillation to concentrate the mind. When your heart is beating irregularly and much faster than usual, leaving you completely exhausted, it does seem to increase your sense of mortality – which at the age of 78 is never very far away anyway. So maybe if I don't get down to writing this now, I may never have the opportunity, and I would like at least my grandchildren to know something about my life.

It began in April 1941. It shouldn't have done, but my heavily pregnant mother was (apparently) out in the back garden chopping wood and that advanced my appearance in this world by about six weeks – small, with no fingernails or toenails, but I managed to survive. It was, of course, the middle of the Second World War. My father, Edward, by then was serving in the North African desert, and *The Times* was reporting that German tanks had been repulsed at Tobruk. My father was a Regimental Sergeant Major in the Royal Corps of Signals by then, and he resisted suggestions that he should apply for a commission, realizing that he was earning more as a Senior NCO than he would get as a Second Lieutenant. He had spent a harrowing couple of days on the Dunkirk beaches in 1940, overseeing the embarkation of the men under his command, and my mother was convinced that it was that terrible experience which changed him from the outgoing, enterprising young man she had married into someone to whom a secure home and job were of first importance. He rarely spoke about the war to us in later years and never about Dunkirk.

In civilian life he was a bank clerk with the old Westminster Bank, a job to which he returned after the war, eventually becoming a branch manager. He seems to have come from quite a prosperous background. His grandfather, Samuel Keene, had been a successful corn factor and was a member also of the Baltic Exchange in the City of London. He had lived in a large property in Barnes, near Richmond, known as Mill Lodge, which many years later was to become Harrods' sports and leisure centre. It was his son Archibald, born to Samuel's second wife, who was my paternal grandfather. Archibald was described on my father's birth certificate as 'of independent means'.

He married May Barrett, the daughter of a Royal Navy warrant engineer, in May 1912 when he was 27, and my father was born almost seven months later. I know nothing about the story of their marriage, but it is difficult to avoid speculating, given that timescale. My father was the eldest of five children, all boys, but not long after the birth of the youngest, the family was split up. Archibald died of stomach cancer in 1922 when my father was nine. We know that by 1925 his mother, May, was in the King Edward VII Sanatorium in Midhurst, Sussex, a hospital for tuberculosis sufferers, and she then disappears from the records. What is also known is that the two youngest children were placed in an orphanage and the older three were split up and cared for by various of Archibald's step-brothers and step-sisters. It cannot have been a happy time. But there was enough money for my father to be sent to Mill Hill School in North London to be privately educated.

My mother, Lilian, had been one of a large family and had met my dad when he came in to the post office branch where she worked. They married shortly before the war broke out. She seems to have had a less troubled background. Her father, Herbert Conway, was a motor engineer from Fulham. He had married a woman whose family originated somewhere in the Dundee area of Scotland. Annie Robb Thomson had had a colourful upbringing – the only one of my grandparents still alive when I was born, she would describe how as a youngster she would ride cows bareback across fields. As an adult, she had worked as a stewardess on ocean-going liners, an adventurous thing to have done at that time. By the time I knew her, she was a formidable old lady, dressed usually in widow's black. There came a time in my young boyhood when I reckoned I could run faster than her and escape up the garden, so I said something rude to her and set off. I was right that I could run faster, but I ran out of garden, was caught and duly spanked. She and Herbert had five children, three girls and two boys. The oldest, Edie, was unmarried and treated me with great kindness. Years later, when I was about 12, she took me on my first foreign holiday to a small hotel in Dinard in Brittany. Using my limited knowledge of French, we hired a couple of bikes with fat red tires, and the locals were treated to the sight of one large lady and one small boy pedalling against the wind along narrow coastal roads. The youngest sister was Vi, who was married to a member of an RAF bomber crew. He, sad to say, went missing in action, leaving a widow and a small daughter.

My mother was the middle one amongst the sisters. She and my father married in 1937 when she was 21 and he 24. Neither had been to university.

I can't claim to remember much about the war. I was only four when it ended. Indeed, by the time I was born the London Blitz had more or less finished. It was only in mid-1944 that the V1 rockets started to come over. I can remember being put to bed several times in a small cupboard under the stairs which were presumably thought to give some added protection. Later, the protection became more purpose-built – I have a distinct recollection of crouching under a metal protective table, a Morrison shelter, in our dining room and hearing the whine of a V1 rocket in the sky. One would listen to the whine, waiting for it to stop, at which point we knew that the engine had cut out and that it would glide down to explode somewhere. I can remember being quite philosophical, waiting for the bang and wondering if I would know anything about it if it hit our house. We weren't an area that suffered badly from bombing, being located on the south-western fringe of London, but occasionally we went out on the morning after a raid to see if we could see what had been hit. Every now and again we would find the odd gap in a row of houses, occupied just by rubble. One could see sometimes that strange vertical cross-section of a house, a wall with a door at first floor level exposed to view.

Inevitably my memories of the immediate post-war period are more vivid. We were living in a small semi-detached house in south-west Middlesex, as it then was. The house was located in Sunbury-on-Thames, but in the northern part furthest from the river. Nowadays the more upmarket southern area is divided from the northern part by the flyover which marks the start of the M3 motorway, but even in my childhood it was evident that the posh part was around Thames Street and its historic buildings. There was still a farm, Manor Farm, in the southern area, together with a park and tennis courts. My father would go off to work in the morning on his bicycle, a machine with drop handlebars, something which seemed to me to be far too racy for my staid father. My mother at that stage stayed at home to run the house and to look after me and my younger brother Andrew, born in 1943. We had no central heating or double-glazing in the house, and ice would form on the inside of my bedroom window during cold winter nights. I can also vividly recollect suffering from chilblains on my ears from the walk to school in one particular winter. We had, of course, no internet or television, no tablets or iPhones, and our main entertainment was derived from the radio. Thrilling programmes like 'Dick Barton – Special Agent' and comedies such as 'Take It From Here' were a must. My brother and I would play table-tennis on the dining room table, and sometimes hockey on the back lawn. The local recreation ground, a treeless mix of grass and mud, provided us with space for very 'coarse' cricket and football.

Every now and then, ice cream would come round, being sold from horse-drawn carts, and the 'rag-and-bone' man, again with a cart pulled by a weary-looking nag and with hoarse indecipherable cries, would appear. In those days milk was delivered daily to the front doorstep in glass bottles which, when emptied, went back onto the doorstep for collection. There were no cars in our street till about 1950, when the first one turned up. My mother knew many of the local traders and shopkeepers, having gone to school locally, and she was quite cynical about their trading methods. I remember her arguing with the local butcher because she reckoned he was adding strips of fat between the rashers of bacon she had asked for. She would count the sacks of coal being delivered by the coalman to make sure that we were not being short-changed. Many things remained rationed during the forties – including eggs and sweets. That must have been why my parents raised and kept chickens in a wire enclosure at the bottom of our garden. As for sweets, I can still remember the sense of wonderment when they ceased to be rationed and I realized that I could buy as many as my pocket money would stretch to.

I think that I must have been an inquisitive child, perhaps a mischievous one. At any rate, at the age of 5 or 6 I managed to burn down three haystacks. We were staying for the summer with relatives of my mother in Scotland. They had a farm near Blairgowrie. It was a very exciting place to be. I rode on tractors, watched fields being mown and the rabbits dashing wildly out as the unmown area got smaller and smaller, and I drank milk squirted straight from the cows. One day I found a box of matches. Experimentally I wondered whether the sort of hay at the corner of a hayrick would burn or not. I thought that if it did, I could just knock it out. I couldn't. The flame spread amazingly fast, licking up the side of the stack and catching the whole rick. I ran inside the farmhouse screaming. I heard the fire engines come, but they couldn't save the rick or the two next to it.

I gathered later that our farming cousin suffered not at all from this episode. The insurers paid up, and the sudden injection of a capital sum into the farm gave it a boost from which it never looked back.

The following year saw my inquisitiveness take a different form. We were staying for our summer holiday in a boarding house in Dovercourt, Essex. This time it was a fire extinguisher which interested me. I wondered how it worked. I found out. Foam gushed everywhere and it couldn't be stopped. The mess was widespread and I was in the doghouse again.

My schooling began at a small private infants' school down near the river in Sunbury. There I was taught vital things like how to tie my shoelaces and how to sing various traditional songs – 'The Minstrel Boy', 'Hearts of Oak', 'Bonnie Dundee' and 'Men of Harlech' amongst them. They remain with me still. They also discovered that I was short-sighted. I was carted off to an optician's in Kingston-on-Thames, where that discovery was confirmed and I was prescribed NHS glasses with almost round metal frames, so that I looked rather like Harry Potter. I hated having to wear glasses. They were a constraint on enjoying playing cricket, because one felt vulnerable, and a barrier to playing rugby. One also, of course, got called names like 'Four Eyes' by other schoolboys. Only after cataract operations in my late sixties was I able to go about my normal life without spectacles.

The glasses did aid my reading, which I did voraciously. My diet included many comics of the time: *Beano, Dandy, Wizard, Hotspur* and eventually the one which adults saw as more worthy, the *Eagle*. All this improved my reading skills and I have never since taken the view that it matters twopence what kids read, so long as they read something.

Eventually I moved on to another day school when I was about 7 or 8 in age. This one, sited near Hampton station, was, I realize in retrospect, really a crammer to make sure that its boys – it was all male – passed the 11 plus examination. Denmead School seemed to be staffed largely by young masters fresh out of the armed forces. One drove an Alfa Romeo sports car in which it was a great thrill to be given a lift. Still, the school did its job. I passed the 11 plus exam with some success and got into my first choice school, Hampton Grammar School. Sitting the 11 plus exam was made particularly memorable because on one of the two days over which it took place, there was a slight disturbance when an anxious-looking teacher came into the room and spoke in hushed tones to the colleague who was invigilating. We discovered later that King George VI had just died. It was 6 February 1952.

Hampton was an old foundation dating from the final years of the reign of Mary Tudor, but by the twentieth century it had become part of the state sector as a voluntary aided school. Some time after I left it, it went independent, but in the early 1950s it was a state grammar school, all boys, with no fees and no boarders, and into which one could only get by passing the 11 plus. Its headmaster when I arrived was a humourless martinet called George Whitfield, who eventually took holy orders. He was rumoured to have caned his sons when he caught them smoking. But the masters generally were very committed and included several who were real characters. One unfortunate teacher was the music teacher, who simply could not keep any sort of order in the class and who was treated (I can see in retrospect) cruelly by the boys. His nickname was Goathead, and I have no idea now what his real name was. He wore a stained tweed suit and had fingers yellow with nicotine from smoking. Sadly, the result was that few of us learned any music or to appreciate any form of classical music. I was into my late twenties before I began to realize what musical delights were available in opera and classical music. It was hearing the Queen of the Night's aria from *The Magic Flute* on the car radio one day which brought home to me the wonders of which the human voice was capable. My musical tastes have since become quite catholic – I find that I enjoy jazz and pop, and more recently classical music. Let me return, however, to those schooldays.

I didn't seem to be much good at the sciences, and so as my school years went by I concentrated on history and English. Meanwhile, Whitfield's heavy hand provoked a number of minor acts of rebellion amongst the pupils – things like explosive caps under the masters' chairs in morning assembly. When the 1955 General Election came along, the school had its own mock election. Whitfield banned a proposed Communist Party slate from running for election, so they renamed themselves the Radical Socialists. Theirs was easily the most entertaining campaign, with processions through the school accompanied by a drummer and other musicians, and chanting as they went. They succeeded in coming a good second in the mock election, the Conservatives winning as had always been likely in a largely middle-class school.

The leader of the Radical Socialists was Rigas Doganis, who at one time was my patrol leader in the school scout troop, and who at one of our summer camps in Devon responded to a dare by running naked from our tent to the nearby woods about 200 metres away and then back again. I didn't see him for many years after the end of our school days, until much to my surprise I found myself having to cross-examine him as an expert witness at a planning inquiry into a proposed runway extension at Luton Airport. By then I was a barrister and he was a highly respected aviation economist – indeed, eventually he became in turn the Chairman/CEO of Olympic Airways and a director of EasyJet. He also became and remains a firm friend.

One of the things to be said in favour of George Whitfield as headmaster is that he took the initiative in starting a school boat club. That made good sense. We were within easy reach of the

Thames, and we came to an arrangement for the use of the boathouse of the Molesey Boat Club. I was persuaded to be a cox, since I was in those days still small enough and light enough for the job. It was a satisfying if stressful role – stressful because the cox steering the boat has the responsibility for avoiding other craft, turning it in quite narrow stretches of river and not getting either the boat or the oars ('blades') into contact with the bank. It also meant that I had to learn to project my voice, since the cox's instructions have to be heard along the full length of a rowing eight over the noise of the wind and water and of the rowing itself. I practised voice-throwing by cycling along quiet country roads nearby, where I could shout without being seen or heard by others. In later life I wondered sometimes if this had helped me in making sure that I could be heard as an advocate.

One of the active members of the boat club was Richard Tilbury ('Tibbles' to his friends). He owned a small rowing dinghy, which he kept in a little wooden boathouse on the Thames near Hampton. He very generously agreed to let me use it, and I would often paddle it to some quiet spot where I could moor and revise for exams or, later during the period between school and university, to try to read some of the material supposed to be studied before starting the degree course. I'm not sure how much work I got done lolling back in the dinghy, but I certainly came away with a love of boats and water which has stayed with me.

In the latter part of my school years I discovered that I enjoyed debating and other forms of public speaking. It was, I found, nerve-racking before you stood up and started speaking, but once you heard the sound of your own voice, it seemed to get easier. So I proposed motions such as favouring the abolition of National Service in a school debate. Unsurprisingly the school audience was only too pleased to vote for the motion!

Eventually the time came to think about university applications. As neither of my parents had been to university or knew much about the comparative merits of the different institutions, I relied on discussions with the masters at school. They made me hope that it was worth trying for Oxford, and Whitfield suggested Balliol College. I couldn't find out much about it, but I thought I would have a go. My history master in the sixth form, Ernie Badman, a short, tubby but ferocious individual, was hugely supportive and gave up a lot of time to widen the area of my historical knowledge by one-to-one tuition. I owe him a lot.

I wasn't sure what degree subject I should apply for. Whitfield saw me in his study to discuss this. There was no mention of PPE. I hadn't heard of it, and I'm not sure that he had. He clearly wasn't convinced of my intellectual abilities. He said 'you'll find it easier to get into Oxford to read law than to read history. You can always change courses once you are there'. It may have been true then that there was less demand for law courses than for history, but it wouldn't be true today, when vocational subjects are over-subscribed. But I took his advice and applied to read law, with Balliol as my first choice of college. I sometimes wonder what would have happened in my later life, had I applied to read history or PPE. It was a life-shaping decision.

2

Oxford

I was a modest, good-humoured boy. It is Oxford that has made me insufferable.

MAX BEERBOHM

So I found myself in Oxford one December day in 1958, awaiting the scholarship exam and the interview. It was bitterly cold. The room in Balliol's front quad in which I was accommodated was heated only by a tiny gas fire, and the wind swept in under the ill-fitting door. I started to wonder why I wanted to come to that place. (I discovered years later that Oxford was well known as a frost pocket, being located in a valley into which the cold air rolled down from the hills, the Chilterns and the Cotswolds, on either side of it.)

I and other applicants filed into the hall of Keble College to do the exams. The architecture of that college seemed to me to be an extravagant piece of folly, like something out of Grimm's *Fairy Tales*. It has since grown on me – a bit. After the exams I had an interview with the then Master of Balliol, Sir David Lindsay Keir, and the junior law fellow, Don Harris. At some stage during the interview they asked me if I would like to discuss anything which had recently been in the news. For an agonizing moment I went a complete blank and couldn't think of anything. Then I remembered that Charles de Gaulle had come to power in France some six months previously after the failure of successive French governments to get a grip on the Algerian crisis. So I talked about the problems of democratic government in France, with the frequent changes of government, expressing views largely derived from discussions with the history masters at Hampton, and that seemed to suffice. A short time later I heard that I hadn't won a scholarship but I was being offered a commoner's place. So up to Balliol I went in October 1959.

Oxford was at first a rather bewildering place. I knew no-one else in my year at Balliol. Four or five others had gone from Hampton to Oxford that year, but nearly all were scientists, and we scarcely met.

The only other exception was Neil Stacy, who later became a successful actor. He was reading history at Magdalen, which seemed a long way away from Broad Street where Balliol was located. The Balliol intake that year was, of course, all male – women weren't admitted to Balliol as undergraduates until twenty years later. The intake seemed to be composed about half from public schools and half from grammar schools, especially ones in the north. The former often seemed to know several others from their former school, which added to their apparent self-confidence.

Probably a bigger distinction was between those who, like me, had come more or less straight from school, and those who had done National Service, the common name for a form of compulsory military service for eighteen months or two years. 1959 was a change-over period: National Service had been abolished for those born after 1 October 1939, but it was a gradual wind-down, and some of those required to do it had been able to delay their period of service. So some of those arriving at Oxford in the autumn of 1959 were not only a couple of years older than 18-year-olds like me but had also seen military service in places like Cyprus. They had fired weapons and they knew far more about life and especially women than the rest of us did. Most of us who had come straight from school were, by present-day standards, remarkably inexperienced about sex, although of course we pretended otherwise.

Gradually I found my feet. The two law tutors at Balliol differed radically. The more senior, Theo Tylor, was an eminent academic lawyer, something all the more remarkable because he was blind. He was not, however, a good teacher of others. His chosen method at tutorials was to try to drum into his students his own particular theories on such abstruse topics as Mistake in Contract, rather than trying to stimulate some original thought on the part of the undergraduate. In contrast, thank heavens, Don Harris, a young New Zealander and former Rhodes Scholar, was mainly concerned with making us think or at least trying to do so. My eventual success in my degree was largely due to him.

Oxford was then, as it still is, full of student societies and clubs, most with an impressive list of outside speakers appearing each term. I was by now getting interested in politics. All the main parties had their student bodies in Oxford and there was no problem in joining more than one, which is what I did in order to hear the speakers. My political ideas were still very uninformed and as the October 1959 election approached, I was quite unsure as to which party to support. I wouldn't be able to vote, being only 18, since at that time the minimum voting age was 21, but it still seemed to me that I should try to make up my mind. My parents were staunch Conservatives, with the *Daily Telegraph* the main newspaper in the house. I was now able to have access to a much wider range of newspapers, and I watched the televised election broadcasts.

There didn't seem a lot of difference between the policies of the two main parties. These were the days of Butskellism, the term applied to the policies aimed at the middle ground of politics, with no hint of the marked divisions which were to come with Margaret Thatcher and Michael Foot. A lot seemed to turn on the character of the individual party leaders, therefore, and I found Harold Macmillan more persuasive and reassuring than

Hugh Gaitskell, who came across as a bit petulant. On such fragile foundations I made my choice – as probably did many in the electorate, since Macmillan was returned to office with an overall majority of 100. I had begun to wonder about combining a political with a legal career, as some MPs did at that time. As those first few terms at Oxford passed, I went to meetings of all three main political parties and eventually decided to get involved more deeply with the Conservative one – the Oxford University Conservative Association known as OUCA. (There was, I discovered later, a national body of such university societies, going by the unfortunate abbreviation FUCUA, the Federation of University Conservative and Unionist Associations.) In my eyes, OUCA was attractive because its leading figures advocated what would later become known as 'wet' Tory policies – emphasis on social welfare, support for colonial independence and high employment through Keynesian economic policies – and its activists called themselves Tory Radicals. They included people like Tony Newton, later a government minister, Phillip Whitehead, who later changed parties and became a Labour MP and MEP, Alan Haselhurst and David Madel, both later Conservative MPs. David was and remains a good friend.

The range of speakers both at the societies and at the Oxford Union, the main debating body of the university, was astonishing. Harold Wilson came when Shadow Chancellor of the Exchequer. At that stage in his career he was extremely dull, not having developed the style of repartee and quips which he used effectively when Labour party leader. Macmillan came to the Oxford Union in the autumn of 1959, to be faced with a surprise motion for an adjournment because of the Report on the deaths at the Hola camp in colonial Kenya. The motion was moved by Phillip Whitehead, an officer of the Union and a splendidly bearded figure. 'Supermac' was heard to mutter that in his day officers of the Union didn't have beards. One also had the experience of hearing consummate debaters like Jeremy Thorpe, Michael Foot, Lord Longford and even more extreme figures like Enoch Powell, Sir Oswald Mosley and Konni Zilliacus.

What all this contact with leading politicians, as well as with judges, QCs, leading journalists and writers, brought home to us was the discovery that such worldly success did not necessarily mean that these people were brighter than we were. Some seemed to be, but others seemed not. What they had over us was experience of the world. But it meant that we learned that there need not be any real limits to what we might achieve. To a teenager from a grammar school and a modest suburban background, it was like being taken to a mountain top and shown the promised land lying beyond. Our horizons opened up enormously.

Oxford very much confirmed my enthusiasm for public speaking. I was still very inexperienced and wasn't a great success in debates at the Oxford Union. But I also took part in law moots – mock legal arguments as if before a court – and found that my initial nerves vanished once I started arguing. So I decided to take the risk of trying for the Bar as a career and I became a student member of the Inner Temple, one of the four Inns of Court to which every barrister must belong. In those days one still had to eat twelve dinners a year at the Inn in Central London. I had no car, but a friend who was also an Inner Temple student and an Oxford undergraduate did have, and he would drive us both there and back. Thinking about it now, I realize that he must have been well over any sensible alcohol limit by the time of the return journey. But there was far less traffic on the roads in those days, it was late at night and the breathalyser was still in the future.

I took an active part in student politics at Oxford and in early 1962 in my third year I was elected Chairman of OUCA. I was very fortunate in the list of cabinet ministers prepared to come to speak that term: Iain Macleod, Henry Brooke, Lord Home and others, but above all, the then Prime Minister Harold Macmillan. He came in February and we took him before the meeting to dinner in the Mitre Hotel, at that time more upmarket than it is now. A lavish meal had been prepared, including smoked salmon and pheasant, but Supermac (as he was being described in the tabloids) could not eat any of it because of nerves. I was amazed that such an accomplished politician, totally in control at that time of the House of Commons, should be nervous before speaking to an audience of students. The lesson I took from it was useful: it confirmed that one should not worry too much if one felt tense and anxious before standing up to speak.

After the meeting, Macmillan chatted over a drink to a few of us back in a private room at the Mitre. He told us how Jack Kennedy rang him every day on the transatlantic scrambler phone, and called him 'Uncle Harold'. He described the disastrous May 1960 Paris summit meeting with Krushchev who performed 'like Micawber' and spoke for three-quarters of an hour, complaining about the American spy plane. Eisenhower just sat there saying 'Waal, I dunno'. De Gaulle retorted to Krushchev, saying that his country was overflown all the time by spy satellites. De Gaulle, Macmillan said, was always accompanied by a supply of blood in case of an attack, the blood having to be kept in a fridge. Despite the failure of that summit, Macmillan's view was that there would eventually be a negotiated agreement with the Russians so long as the West remained patient. He foresaw the Soviet Union becoming more like a capitalist society, and stressed Krushchev's Ukrainian background which made him more Eurocentric. When Macmillan had been in Vienna as Foreign Secretary in 1955 for the negotiations on the Austrian treaty, the Americans had tapped the phone line of Molotov, the Russian foreign minister. It was, said Macmillan, to no avail. All they learned was that Molotov's daughter was learning the violin.

Macmillan came across as warm and of course stylish, and he was very much at ease talking to a small group of undergraduates.

He certainly charmed me, and I always enjoyed hearing him speak. He was a real performer.

There was, as is well known, an element of play-acting in his performances. Many years later, when he was long retired as a politician, he came to a dinner in hall at Balliol, where he had been an undergraduate, the dinner being in his honour. He was by then walking with a stick and seemed very frail. When it came to his turn to speak at the end of the meal, he rose slowly and apparently painfully. He then stood there silently, and gradually the tension built. We all began to think that the old boy had finally lost it. But eventually he began, slowly at first but soon with more vigour, and before long it became clear that the whole hesitant episode had been contrived. It was a masterly performance.

The summer vacations at Oxford were rightly called 'Long'. They provided a great opportunity to travel, even with very little money. In July 1961 I went overland as a pillion passenger on a friend's motor scooter all the way from this country to the then Yugoslavia – via Ostend, Aachen, Köln, Koblenz, Nuremberg, Regensburg, Passau, Vienna and into what is now Slovenia at Maribor. Three things stick in my memory about that trip: first, standing on the podium at Nuremberg where the Nazi rallies took place, trying to imagine the scene then in comparison to the weed and grass-infested steps now; secondly, the stunningly beautiful lakes, streams and waterfalls at Plitvice in what is now Croatia; and thirdly, the discovery that there is a limit of about one hour on the time that the human posterior can withstand the jolting of a motor scooter's pillion without needing a rest!

The following year I went with a group to Berlin. The infamous wall had been in position for less than a year, but there was already a heart-rending collection of wreaths and tributes along the base of it on the West Berlin side, marking where East Germans trying to escape to the west had been shot by their own security forces. What a regime that had to use a wall, barbed wire and bullets to keep its own people in their country!

The most significant event in my time at Oxford was meeting a PPE undergraduate at St Hugh's College called Gillian Lawrance. She was obviously intelligent and very attractive, and I soon discovered how interesting she was. My feelings seemed to be reciprocated and eventually we became engaged. In 1965, after we had both left university, we got married, an event to which I shall return.

I managed to my surprise to obtain an unviva'd First in my Final BA exams. This in turn brought various very welcome scholarships and awards. Balliol, Oxford University and the Inner Temple all helped me financially in this way. I stayed in Oxford for a fourth year to do a post-graduate law degree, the Bachelor of Civil Law. Doing that achieved two things: it exempted me from some of the Bar exams I would eventually have to take and it meant an extension to my university grant for another year. Apart from those sources of income, I was dependent financially on what I could earn in the vacations. Those were sometimes fun. One involved helping in a boatyard on the Thames, rigging sailing dinghies and preparing motor boats, all for hiring out. When it rained, there were no customers and I could read happily.

3

An American Interlude

[President Kennedy and I] talked of many things, including Great Britain's role in the world as an honest broker. I agreed with him, when he said that no nation could be more honest, and he agreed with me, when I chaffed him, and said that no nation could be broker.

PETER COOK as HAROLD MACMILLAN in 'Beyond the Fringe'

I finished my time in Oxford at the end of the summer term 1963 and I was then lucky enough to be awarded one of Balliol's Coolidge 'Pathfinder' Awards, of which there were eight each year. These had been initiated in the post-war period by Bill Coolidge, a New Englander, who recognized that the shortage of dollars in the UK was such that travel to the USA was virtually impossible. He financed the awards for travel and study. Many years later the scheme was taken over and financed by William Westerman. It was necessary for a candidate for one of these awards to put forward some form of project to be pursued over a period of two or three months, though these could be couched in quite general terms, as mine certainly was. I stated that I wanted to study the legal and political system in the USA. That enabled me to plan a trip more or less around the whole country. We eight were enormously fortunate. We were given a long list of people, mostly Balliol graduates, in the USA who would accommodate us for a few days, plus a limited amount of cash per week and a car between two or three of us. We began by assembling in Bill Coolidge's house at Topsfield, some distance north of Boston, to which I drove from the airport in the evening rush hour. For a young man with limited experience of driving on UK roads just sufficiently to have passed my driving test, it was a terrifying experience to find oneself on a freeway with four lanes of traffic each way. Somehow I survived.

Before leaving Topsfield, I saw the impressive facilities of the Harvard Law School and we were kitted out with suits from the Harvard Co-op (or 'Coop', as we found it called). Then we were away. Three of us headed south to New York City, and then into the rural parts of New York State, followed by Pennsylvania. I still remember seeing the Amish there, people who reject much of modern technology and whom we saw driving their horses and carriages and wearing simple clothes. But the highlight of this part of the trip was Washington DC. We had a contact in a Senator's office, which turned out to be staffed by (in our eyes) remarkably young people. This was the era of Jack Kennedy as

President, and all of Washington seemed vibrant and youthful, especially in contrast to the UK where the Macmillan administration was in its final faltering months. Our accommodation there was provided by Nicholas de B. Katzenbach, a graduate of Balliol and now the Deputy Attorney-General of the United States. Later, after Bobby Kennedy decided to run for the US Senate, he became the Attorney-General. I remember discussing with him one evening, as we sat on the veranda of his Georgetown house, the merits of the British and American systems of appointing/electing judges. One of the other Coolidge men staying there, Terry Cooper, a chemistry graduate, took me to task afterwards for arguing with the Deputy Attorney-General of the USA. I said I thought that Katzenbach as a lawyer himself took argument like that in his stride.

Virginia came next, where Terry, a mild non-political man, quite shocked a group of Daughters of the American Revolution by his moderately liberal views. But what a beautiful state! Driving down through the Carolinas we started to see more and more evidence of racial segregation – signs saying 'Whites only' on public lavatories, cafes and so on. Our trip took us down through Atlanta and then west to New Orleans, where we visited the French Quarter and heard some traditional jazz. The drive from there across Louisiana, the vast stretches of Texas (via Dallas, not yet of notoriety) and into New Mexico seemed endless, but we eventually got to a beautiful ranch in the foothills of the Rockies, where we rode horses and generally relaxed.

Our appreciation of the Grand Canyon was slightly dulled by the fact that we couldn't find anywhere to stay and so spent a sleepless night in the car. We felt that we had to go on to see Las Vegas, which had more neon lighting and tacky signs than I thought possible – the wee Kirk O'The Heather chapel still springs to mind. Los Angeles seemed mainly freeways and lacking in a centre, more a collection of suburbs linked by roads, but at Santa Barbara to the north we did stay on a dude ranch owned by the Sedgwicks, who were very hospitable. Their daughter, Edie, was later to find a degree of fame as the muse for Andy Warhol. She died age 28, only eight years after I met her. San Francisco was a knock-out. There we parted company and I went on alone by train, taking the Shasta Daylight Special up the west coast to Portland, Oregon. That was a truly memorable ride, passing through mountains and forest, with tumbling rivers and waterfalls, a beautiful wilderness which gave me an enduring passion for that part of the USA. That was enhanced by my time in Seattle, where I stayed on one of the small islands.

From Seattle I took a train east, right across the northern part of the USA to Chicago, awe-inspiring as we passed through the Rockies but then increasingly tedious as we traversed mile after mile of the Great Plains – waving wheat field after wheat field. The train was full of young American students heading back to college, with that sort of assertiveness which J. D. Salinger describes in *The Catcher in the Rye*. After a change of trains in Chicago (all I saw of that apparently splendid city) I got back to Boston, from where I flew home.

It was an amazing experience, one which I was extraordinarily lucky to have. It left me with an abiding love for the American open spaces, a lack of affection for the small towns dominated by billboards and outlets, and a strong respect for the country's democratic institutions. That still remains, despite the election of Donald Trump. But Ogden Nash got the billboards right:

> I think that I shall never see
> A billboard lovely as a tree.
> Perhaps, unless the billboards fall,
> I'll never see a tree at all.

While in the States I had seen on television the civil rights demonstrations, including the great March on Washington at the end of August 1963, at which Martin Luther King gave his memorable 'I have a Dream' speech. It seemed that, under Jack and Robert Kennedy, things were going to change, albeit somewhat cautiously. At least that year JFK had given his passionate support to a Civil Rights Bill. It came, therefore, as a shattering blow only a few months later in November to hear that he had been shot and then that he had died.

4

Bar Pupillage, and Marriage

'In my youth', said his father, 'I took to the law,
And argued each case with my wife;
And the muscular strength which it gave to my jaw
Has lasted the rest of my life.

LEWIS CARROLL

Back in the UK, I finished my bar exams, and I was called to the Bar by the Inner Temple in April 1964. That October I began a pupillage, a form of traineeship, with Denis Henry (later Lord Justice Henry) at 2 Crown Office Row, chambers which subsequently moved to Fountain Court. The pupillage had been arranged for me through the Balliol connection, Denis being a graduate of the college. He, like most of the members of chambers, had a very varied practice. Nothing seemed beyond his reach: crime, divorce, tax, family law, mainstream contract and tort – all came his way, and reading his papers and listening to his advocacy was an invaluable education. At the same time I noted how his wide range of legal subjects meant that he was working flat out, night after night and weekend after weekend. I began to wonder if a more specialist part of the Bar might be more attractive. Denis' success at the Bar was all the more remarkable because he suffered at times from a form of stutter.

The chambers were located in the Temple, that part of London which had once been occupied by the Knights Templar, but their wealth eventually attracted the attention of Edward II and he dissolved them. Quite soon the lawyers moved in and have remained ever since. The area is still a historic and attractive place. When I first went into it, leaving the noise and the traffic of Fleet Street and the Strand, I was struck by how tranquil it was. Though there were and are cars parked there, there is no through route and Middle Temple Lane, which roughly divides the Inner Temple from the Middle Temple, is cobbled. The street lighting is still gas, and in the 1960s those lights were lit each evening at dusk by a man who came round with a long pole. Today there are little clocks in each light. But the area is often used for filming scenes meant to be set in the eighteenth and nineteenth centuries. Apart from the Inner Temple and the Middle Temple, there is also an Outer Temple. This, however, consists only of a long covered passageway, part of which has a glazed roof, leading from the Strand into the Middle Temple, together with a single set of chambers.

Fleet Street, which runs along the northern side of the Inner Temple, was in the early 1960s still the centre of the national newspaper industry, with papers such as the *Daily Telegraph* and *Daily Mail* amongst many others. Newspaper vans were a common sight. Some of the bars in the area were frequented by both lawyers and journalists, who in establishments such as El Vino's could exchange stories and gossip. There was a small private club called the Wig and Pen opposite the Royal Courts of Justice, and I was persuaded to become a life member. It wasn't a good investment – the club closed some years later and it is now a Thai restaurant.

In addition to his other varied work, Denis also did a little planning law work, that is to say, appearing at planning inquiries before an inspector. These inquiries adopt the approach of an informal court case, though invariably with expert witnesses – highway engineers, planners, architects – rather than lay witnesses of events. While I was his pupil, Denis was briefed to appear at a public inquiry in Oxford on behalf of Balliol, which had an objection to a minor part of the Development Plan for the city. He was only going to need to be there for one day when the College's objection was heard, but the experienced senior clerk in chambers, Cyril Batchelor, got me a noting brief for the whole duration of the inquiry, which turned out to be eight days in all. For this I was to be paid £5.10s.0d per day, equivalent in modern currency to £5.50, though worth far more then than now.

This inquiry was a turning point in my life. The main issue arose over a proposal by the Oxfordshire County Council and Oxford City Council to build a new road through the unspoilt landscape of Christchurch Meadow. This was to be a relief road, taking traffic off the congested High Street. The local authorities publicly regretted the damage to the scenic beauty of the open space, but the conventional wisdom was that you could only persuade drivers to use the preferred alternative if it was constructed sufficiently close to the road one sought to relieve. Many Inner Relief Roads had been and were to be built in our towns and cities in compliance with this thinking, and to my regret I was later responsible for promoting such a road in Colchester on behalf of the local authority.

But in Oxford the Oxford Preservation Trust objected, raised enough money to brief an experienced QC and an expert witness, and pursued its objection vigorously. Its expert witness was Colin Buchanan, a traffic engineer and planner, who had led a group which had just produced *Traffic in Towns*, sometimes known indeed as the Buchanan Report. He introduced to the Oxford inquiry the concept of 'traffic management measures', whereby one could take positive steps to deter drivers from using the old route, rather than by leaving it to unfettered choice, and consequently the relief road could be built further out. That approach has now become conventional wisdom, but in 1965 it was obviously a novel idea to most of those at the inquiry.

Hearing Professor Buchanan give evidence was an eye-opener, and I decided that this sort of work was much more interesting than conventional litigation. The road was never built through Christchurch Meadow. The planning inspector, and later the Secretary of State, accepted Buchanan's approach.

As I came towards the end of my pupillage with Denis Henry, he explained to me that at least one member of chambers thought that I was too opinionated and so I would not be kept on as a tenant in chambers. Though this was a blow, he knew that I had become interested in planning work and promised to try to find a planning set of chambers which might take me. Many years later I was somewhat comforted by the discovery that roughly half of Denis' pupils had not been taken on as tenants and the unfortunates included Derry Irvine (later a very successful QC and Lord Chancellor), Sir Christopher Bellamy (later the UK judge at the EU Court of First Instance) and a number of other distinguished judges and QCs. Choosing people for tenancies – and any other job, as I later found to my cost – is a very fallible process. I was also comforted at the time of my rejection at 2 Crown Office Row by the award in 1965 of Oxford's Eldon Scholarship, something which had not been won by someone from Balliol since Tom Bingham (later Lord Bingham of Cornhill).

I was eventually found a place in a mainly planning set, then at 3 Temple Gardens, where I was asked to do a brief pupillage with Richard Yorke, who was largely a commercial and banking specialist. Richard was a flamboyant and generous character, known to Denis Henry because he too had been at Balliol. Richard drove an old, though not vintage, Rolls Royce, had a share in a light aircraft and generally put on quite a lavish show. Such was his generosity that, when I got married a few months later in August 1965, he lent us his Rolls Royce for our honeymoon in the Lake District – a wonderful gift, marred only slightly by the fact that it didn't have a current tax disc. Every time we went through a built-up area, we were on edge in case a policeman spotted the out-of-date disc.

The chambers were small by modern standards, with only about eight members, not all of whom were full-time. The Head of Chambers when I arrived was Charles Schofield QC, a local government law specialist, who was about to hand over to Douglas Frank, who was on the verge of taking silk. Of my vintage there was Konrad Schiemann, who became a good friend and who was eventually a Court of Appeal Judge and then later the UK judge at the European Court of Justice at Luxembourg. The chambers could not be described as a leading planning set, but did planning work and, moreover, was about to move physically to new premises in Gray's Inn, just north of Holborn, where there would be much more accommodation. Douglas Frank, as the new Head of Chambers, was clearly on the look-out for possible new members. I was warned by a number of friends at the Bar that, if I went in for a mainly planning practice, I would not get into court very often and so would be unlikely ever to become a judge. That didn't worry me. I couldn't think of anything more boring than sitting on one's backside all day having to listen to other people arguing a case. I wanted to do the arguing. People do, however, change over time.

Gillian and I had been engaged for some time by now, and we decided to plan to marry in August that year. Her parents, Geoff and Peggy Lawrence, were then living in Norwich, where Geoff was the Assistant Collector of Customs for that region. He had had a remarkable career, going into the Customs & Excise at the lowest, clerical, grade and working his way up through the equivalent of executive into administrative civil service grades. He finished as Collector, London Central. Because Gilly was living in Norwich, we decided to marry there and, though neither of us was religious, we chose a church service because of the ceremonial. So we were married on 14 August 1965 in the parish church of Eaton, said to be the only thatched church within a city boundary in England. The service had one unusual feature: as Gilly's wedding dress had gold thread within it, the vicar decided to talk about the inherent value of gold. This produced some critical murmurings from the economists amongst our friends, who clearly disputed his thesis. My best man was Gordon Langley, an old Balliol friend and later a High Court Judge, whom I still see in the Inner Temple. We honeymooned in the

Lake District, staying in a delightful small hotel called The Bridge in the tiny village of Buttermere. The hotel was equipped for walkers, with an efficient drying room for wet boots and clothes, and we did a lot of walking. The hotel keeper was very friendly – when I ordered a bottle of Nuits St Georges one night, mainly because it was the only red wine on the list whose name I was sure I could pronounce, he explained to us that the delivery man for the wines always referred to it as 'newts'. It has remained so for us ever since.

Our married life began in rented rooms in Golders Green, from which we house-hunted. We did so in south-east London, since Gilly's family had connections there, but even in that part of London it was dispiriting. During my pupillage at the Bar, I had managed to earn some money as a law lecturer at University College London, cramming that in to just a day or two per week, and Gillian had just been appointed as a philosophy lecturer there, but we were very hard up. Some estate agents tried, not very successfully, to conceal their amusement when we told them the price range we were looking for. Eventually I decided to try my advocacy skills at a local branch of the Halifax Building Society. I had no earnings at the Bar of significance, but I took along the figures of other members of chambers and said that this was the sort of level of earnings I hoped for in a few years. If I didn't succeed at the Bar, I had a good degree and could always get a university post. So one of my earliest and greatest achievements as an advocate was persuading the Halifax to grant us a mortgage on a Wates maisonette in Lee Green, south-east London. We had virtually no furniture but we managed.

My political views had been changing rapidly in the period since I had left Oxford. I discovered that the Conservative Party out in the real world was not so liberal as its supporters in the university believed. In particular, it seemed to me to be very much a party for the protection of the middle class, despite the fact that it had always persuaded quite a number of working class voters to support it. I was also stunned in October 1963 when, by some mysterious process, the party chose Lord Home to become its leader, albeit as Sir Douglas Home, in succession to Harold Macmillan. At that point, I decided to resign from the party. I had been elected as Senior Vice-Chairman of the national student body, of which Ken Clarke was the Chairman and indeed a friend, and so I wrote to him, telling him of my decision. He was taken aback, but forgiving.

Consequently, when it came to the 1966 election Gilly and I were to be found canvassing the Wates estate on behalf of the Labour Party. I still had a political future in mind as a possibility and joined the Young Fabian Group, part of the Fabian Society. In that capacity I chaired a group studying sentencing policy for adult offenders, which eventually in 1967 produced a pamphlet entitled *The Adult Criminal*. It emphasized the limitations of imprisonment and the benefits, both social and economic, of community penalties such as probation. My experience since that time, especially as a judge, has only served to confirm me in those early views. Eventually I became Chairman of the Young Fabian Group. It brought me into contact with a number of leading members of the Labour Party, including Shirley Williams and Roy Hattersley. He on one occasion explained to us youngsters that there was in politics 'a time for the thumb in the eye and the knee in the groin'. Presumably only occasionally.

Gilly and I had not felt that we could afford to start a family immediately after marriage, and so it was just the two of us who drove our new Mini to Czechoslovakia in the summer of 1966, just two years (as it turned out) before the Prague uprising and the Russian invasion. We found the countryside disappointing, with very little town and country planning, such as separating industry and homes, which surprised me in an ostensibly planned economy. The people in the villages seemed sullen. Prague was very different. There was already a sense of restlessness. We had with us an English–Czech phrasebook, bought at the left-wing bookshop, Collets, in London and with this we broke the ice with the locals we met in the bars. When they saw the phrase 'Tell me, Mr Novotny, do you get a bonus for exceeding the norm on your collective?' they would roar with laughter and buy us yet another of their excellent beers. They were not reticent in expressing their views. Some were serious views, but one man, to whom I explained that I was (now) a socialist, retorted that he was a conservative – 'Winston Churchill, puff, puff', accompanied by the cigar-smoking gestures. We felt so saddened two years later to be watching the tanks rolling through those same streets.

Our daughter Harriet had been born in January 1968, which as any parent knows meant profound change in our lives. Even with some broken nights, she was our delight, and we hung on her early words and achievements. Gilly took maternity leave but kept her university job. Harriet was joined just over two years later by a brother, Edward, born in May 1970. By now we had moved from Lee Green to Blackheath, mainly because we wanted more space and a garden, and so we traded up to a large semi-detached house. Blackheath was an attractive area, though without in those days any easy access to a tube line, with the result that commuting to central London involved either a very slow road journey through south-east London or a crowded and unreliable train. Nonetheless, it was a pleasant area to start raising our family.

5

Life at the Bar – Early Days

No brilliance is needed in the law
Nothing but common-sense and relatively clean fingernails.
JOHN MORTIMER

'Now you're a member of chambers, Sir, you'll have to buy yourself a bowler hat.' This was the senior clerk, Jack Bronsden, to me, a 24-year-old brand new member of this small set of barristers' chambers in London.

'Oh Jack, do I really need to? Why do I have to have a bowler?'

'Well, sir, you need something to raise to the judges when you meet them in the street.'

I couldn't see myself wearing a bowler hat. I had never worn any sort of hat in my life other than a school cap, and so I prevaricated. Fortunately, within six months of that conversation, by one of those strange shifts of fashion, virtually nobody at the

Bar was wearing a bowler any more. Some of the judges still did, and the tall figure of Lord Justice Harman could sometimes be seen wearing a top hat as he stalked between Lincoln's Inn and the law courts. But he, as in many things, was an exception.

The conversation I had with Jack Bronsden typified the apparent relationship between barristers and their clerks. The clerks, especially the Senior Clerk of a set of chambers, would in effect tell the younger barristers what they were to do. 'You're in Hillingdon Mags tomorrow, Sir', and off you would go to the magistrates court the next day. But the nominally superior status of the barrister required the word 'Sir' (or Miss or Madam, in the rare cases where it was appropriate) to be tacked on the end. I never did National Service, but it sounded to me like the way a seasoned Sergeant Major would address an inexperienced young officer. It was in the same spirit that Jack told me one day that the new suit I was wearing, that I regarded as the height of fashion, was quite unsuitable for wearing in chambers. So that was that.

I learned that barristers' clerks were a strange breed. At that time paid a percentage of what their principals earned, they were at best a mix of market trader and diplomat. They could haggle with solicitors on the phone about fees they were negotiating – 'I never let Mr Freeman out of chambers for less than £. . . a day, Sir' – sometimes wildly exaggerating the experience of a barrister they were seeking to persuade a solicitor to brief, and then the next day taking the senior partner of a big City firm of solicitors to lunch with complete aplomb. Many senior clerks made a lot of money, being paid usually a percentage of chambers' earnings, originally about 10 per cent. Nobody quite knew how they were recruited. Some seemed to work on a hereditary principle. Almost none had been to university in those days. Most started as very junior clerks, heaving books to and from court, making coffee and running errands, all on a low salary, but with the prospect of big rewards in due course.

I never resented the slice of my earnings which went to my senior clerk. He held much of my career and certainly much of my financial welfare in his hands. I was very fortunate, because for nearly all my years at the Bar I had a very talented clerk, Leslie Page, who took over at a young age from Jack Bronsden when Jack suddenly died from a heart attack one night.

Although these were mainly planning chambers, one could not confine oneself, as a young junior (a non-QC), to planning work if one wanted a decent income. Fortunately chambers had a number of sidelines. One of the best was the licensing of road haulage vehicles, which at that time needed not merely road tax licences but also a commercial licence, an 'A' or 'B' licence as an operator. Existing hauliers could object to the grant of a new haulage licence or to the extension of an existing one so as to cover new areas of work. They would object principally on the ground that there was no need for such a grant, and the issue would be decided by a person called the Licensing Authority, who held hearings at which evidence was called and cross-examined on. Our chambers had a retainer from the nationalized haulier, British Road Services, who seemed to object to just about everything. So we got plenty of work at, I believe, 'fifteen and two' (that is, 15 guineas plus 2 guineas) if in London, a bit more outside.

Many of us from several chambers cut our teeth on such work. Regulars included Elizabeth Butler-Sloss (now Baroness), Matthew Thorpe (later a Court of Appeal judge), Peter Singer (later a High Court judge), as well as Richard Yorke and Konrad Schiemann from our chambers. It provided excellent training, because you had to cross-examine on evidence of which you had had no advance notice, often consisting of figures and accounts.

But there was other more conventional litigation, such as building litigation or other contractual disputes. Not all got to court. I had to tell one over-enterprising client, who I think was Iranian, that although his contract had, tucked away in the lengthy and very very small print, a clause giving him the right subsequently to require the other party to purchase whatever multiple of the main contract goods he decided on, the English courts were unlikely to enforce it. He purported to be very shocked, but I learned later that other members of the Bar had given similar advice.

We had quite a few sporting cases. I appeared for John Conteh, world light heavyweight champion, in a dispute with his manager.

John relied on an oral agreement, the manager denied it, and we lost. The same solicitor brought me a contract claim by Paul Raymond of Raymond's Revuebar and of several soft-porn magazines. His claim arose out of a show called Royalty Follies, involving a large plastic tank on stage, filled with water. In it a young woman wearing a bikini would frolic with two small dolphins, which in due course would remove the bikini. I discovered a trade secret, namely that to achieve this, sardines were placed under the bikini straps! Paul Raymond's problem was that, first, the tank had sprung a leak which had had to be cured by adding plastic struts to it, and secondly the water filter had malfunctioned, leading to murky water. The end result was that the audience got no clear view of the young woman and the show closed early. So Paul Raymond wanted to sue the suppliers of the tank.

I advised him that he had a good claim under the Sale of Goods Act, on the basis that the tank was not fit for the purpose for which it was supplied. All seemed fine until I had to draft the claim, which required me to plead what the purpose was for which the tank had been supplied. I was reluctant to spell out in detail what the tank had been intended for, but as I tried to phrase it in more general terms, I realized that that was not much of an improvement – 'in which a young woman and two dolphins were to perform certain acts' seemed to me to provide too much of a stimulus to the imagination. In the end, I found a formula and, much to my relief, the case eventually settled.

Chambers did a certain amount of local government law. One of our members, Harold Parrish, had a retainer from the Local Government Association which paid him a small fee to advise on questions raised by local councils. All they wanted was his opinion, not a host of reasons, and he duly obliged. His standard answer, whatever the question, was 'Yes' or 'No', or if he felt especially loquacious, he would add the words 'in my opinion'! Some of the local government cases concerned elections, and one from the London Borough of Croydon came my way. We ended up before Lord Denning, the Master of the Rolls and, as such, head of the Court of Appeal's civil division. He was very much a judge with an eye for the merits of a case and did not feel over-restricted by the law, which one has to recognize he developed in some very innovative ways. He was Master of the Rolls for some twenty years, an amazingly long time, during which he developed the concept of holding people to their promises if the other party has relied on the promise and also the concept of the deserted wife having an interest in the matrimonial home. He did all this and more in judgments which are a model for others who have to produce judgments – short sentences, expressed in simple but colourful language: 'It was bluebell time in Kent' (Hinz *v.* Berry). Often one could see from his opening sentences who had won or lost the case. One of his most celebrated judgments concerned a householder who had obtained an injunction to stop a cricket club playing cricket which resulted in balls coming into his garden. Denning's judgment began: 'In summertime, village cricket is a delight to everyone', and by the time he had referred to the householder as a 'newcomer', in contrast to the seventy years that cricket had been played on the adjoining green, you knew that the injunction was a dead letter.

Sadly, though in my election petition case where I acted for the Returning Officer I had the law on my side, I didn't have the merits. But I cited to Lord Denning my principal legal authority, a decision from the 1890s which other courts had applied ever since and which, being itself a Court of Appeal decision, was technically binding on him. It was no use. He peered over his half-moon glasses at me and in his charming Hampshire accent said, smiling: 'Oh Mr Keene, that is a very old case. I think we are going to have to make some new law today.' Which he did. What can one do in such a situation, other than subside gracefully?

My first High Court civil trial was one in 1967 in Manchester, when I had only been a barrister for three years. It was not a success. My clients were claiming breach of contract by two companies. They were separately represented by two much more experienced counsel – Ben Hytner, now less well known than his son Nick, the theatre director, and George Carman, who was later to achieve fame in defending Ken Dodd on tax charges and Jeremy Thorpe, the Liberal Party leader, on an attempted murder charge. He also appeared in many libel cases. My performance in the breach of contract case was not enhanced by the fact that my instructing solicitor had entertained me to an excellent but over-alcoholic dinner the evening before the case began. After champagne, wine and brandy, it was only through a mist that I heard him say, as a waiter approached with boxes of cigars, 'never have a Jamaican, dear boy, when you can have a Havana'. Excellent advice, maybe, but the combination of alcohol and cigar meant that I was up for half the night, heaving up into the loo, and by morning possessed of a splitting headache. Ben and George duly disposed of my arguments on the second day in court and then kindly took me to (a non-alcoholic!) lunch. That was my introduction to the friendliness of the provincial Bars.

I did also get the planning inquiry work for which I had been hoping. One of the first came soon after I became a full member of chambers, when I was briefed as the junior to Douglas Frank QC on behalf of Essex County Council to oppose the proposal by the Ministry of Aviation to make Stansted the third London airport. It was the beginning for me of a long involvement in airport inquiries and especially in those concerning the third London airport. Stansted at that time was in aviation terms an insignificant place. It had been a US air force bomber base during the Second World War, and that had left it with the asset of a long and strong runway, greatly underused. The Ministry wanted to get greater use of it. So from December 1965 to February 1966 there was a public inquiry in Chelmsford Town Hall before an independent inspector, a senior partner in a well-known firm of chartered surveyors. I found the aviation and air traffic control evidence fascinating. But the Ministry's case was undermined by an incompetent witness from the Ministry of Transport, who was called to demonstrate that Stansted would be within the drive-time from central London set out by the government as one of the criteria that a new airport, whether at Stansted or elsewhere, must meet. He became very muddled, and even a second attempt at showing that Stansted would comply failed to clarify things. His counsel, Milner Holland QC, was privately furious, as he made clear to us.

In the event, the inspector found that such an airport at Stansted would have very adverse effects on the locality, which could only be outweighed by a national need for the development. No such need, he concluded, had been established at the inquiry. Thus he recommended that the proposal be rejected. The government rejected his recommendation and proposed to go ahead with the scheme. Douglas Frank and I decided, with the backing of our clients, to challenge this in the courts, but we lost.

It was not, however, the end of the story. There was a change of Minister, and Anthony Crosland decided that the case for Stansted had not been adequately investigated. This, as his widow's biography of him makes clear, was a thunderbolt to his civil servants. He decided that there should be a multi-disciplinary commission to consider the need for any location of a third London airport, and he appointed Sir Eustace Roskill, then a High Court judge, to chair it. It had a mix of engineers, planners and economists on it, and was assisted by a substantial research team. It did its own studies and came up with a short list of four sites. Stansted was not one of them. The four included a site on the Foulness Sands (also known as Maplin) just north-east of Southend in Essex and one in the Vale of Aylesbury in Buckinghamshire, around the villages of Cublington and Wing.

The eventual public hearing into the merits of these four sites took place in the basement ballroom of the Piccadilly Hotel in London and continued for many months.

Essex County Council had again briefed Douglas Frank QC and me, our position being in favour of Foulness. The commission's work laid great stress on cost-benefit analysis, which in itself was an advance on previous methods, but did require any decision-maker to take care that the quantifiable merits or demerits of a site did not lead to an under-valuation of the unquantifiable ones. I felt that the issue of travel-time from London and elsewhere to the sites, which could have a notional cost put on it, tended to dominate the issues of landscape, attractive villages and listed buildings, to which it was very difficult to attach a value.

The upshot was that a majority of the Commission recommended Cublington/Wing, but with one of its members, Colin Buchanan, preferring Foulness/Maplin. A new government under Edward Heath went for the latter and an Act of Parliament was passed providing for a third London airport at Maplin. It was, however, an expensive option, because it involved new dedicated road and rail links, and such an investment was scuppered by the oil crisis of 1973 and the three-day week of early 1974. In due course, Stansted reappeared on the scene! I have no doubt that that was because of the presence of the strong, lengthy runway and the reluctance of the civil service to see that asset lying almost idle. The irony is that, when Stansted eventually became the third London airport, it was found that the runway was orientated in a direction which was less than ideal, and so an entirely new runway was substituted. It is a sorry tale.

There were other airport inquiries, at Birmingham (the new terminal building), Southend, Luton and Norwich, but the other large source of work for me in this period came from motorway and trunk road inquiries. One I greatly enjoyed was that into a proposal to extend the M3 motorway southwards from Basingstoke to the M27 at Southampton. This was a time when the Ministry of Transport (as it then was) kept trying to restrict the scope of objections which an inspector could hear at an inquiry, and this led to a great deal of protest and disruption to inquiries. The M3 inquiry took place at Winchester and the protests took a more middle-class form. The wife of the Dean led the whole gathering in prayers for the guidance of the inspector, who clearly felt that he had to go along with this! But there was some disruption, largely because the proposal was to run the motorway through part of the water meadows at Winchester. My clients were the main opponents, being an action group of various smaller groups, as well as Winchester College itself.

The inspector was a kindly retired Major-General, but he had to keep order, and eventually declared that the next person to interrupt the proceedings would be ejected. One of our supporters, a young history master at the College, was undeterred and was then duly ejected. At that point, the Headmaster of the College, John Thorne, who was in the audience, felt that he had to support a member of his staff and so stood up and said so. He too was then ejected, an event which made the national press the next day.

During my time in and around Winchester, I came to know and love the City, its surroundings and the Itchen Valley. I was delighted when in due course the inspector rejected the proposal to route the motorway through the water meadows. I still regard it as one of my favourite achievements. That is despite the fact that the Department of Transport chose as an alternative to put the motorway through the Downs in an uncovered cutting.

I was less successful in trying to oppose various sections of the M25. One case was particularly difficult, the Swanley–Sevenoaks section in the south-eastern part of the circular route. It was difficult because the motorway had already been built as far as Swanley in the north, where an elevated section stopped in midair, pointing southwards. The route had also been approved in the south as far as Sevenoaks, so there was this obvious gap waiting to be filled. Unfortunately, the proposed route was environmentally damaging: it ran through an Area of Outstanding Natural Beauty, Green Belt, high quality farmland and some land of Great Landscape Value. So we did what we could. Our alternative suggestion was a longer route, using the existing M20 and M26. It was about double the distance of the proposed route, but we were helped by the Ministry's decision to call one of its backroom experts who had not given evidence before and who had published articles that gave support to part of our case.

The inspector was an experienced planning QC, George Dobry, who charmed the objectors from Day 1. They had been very worked up initially, but George captivated them, so much so that when his birthday occurred, they gave him a cake and sang 'Happy Birthday to You'! Some of the female members of the action group I represented also had the novel idea of wearing T-shirts, with emblazoned across the chest the words 'This is an Area of Outstanding Natural Beauty'. George was greatly amused. Nonetheless, we lost.

The amount of violent protest at major road inquiries reached a peak in 1976 at one in West Yorkshire, where (for once) I was appearing to promote a new route on behalf of the Ministry. This was the Airedale Trunk Road, intended to relieve the A650 west of Shipley with a dual two-lane road. It produced vehement protests when the inspector, a retired local authority engineer, tried to open the inquiry. There were chants of 'This Inquiry hasn't opened' and attempts to drown the inspector's words. This went on when he called on me to open the case for the Ministry. I had the benefit of a microphone, but then a crowd of people surged forwards to try to grab it. I was assisted at the inquiry by another member of chambers, David Mole, later a circuit judge. He manfully sought to put himself between my microphone and the mob, and told me afterwards that he had found himself locked in a sort of rugger scrum, where his opponent was muttering in his ear: 'Come on, lad, give up. You can't win. I'm a pig farmer.'

The inspector adjourned to the next day and, against our urgings, decided to continue the inquiry then in private, merely inviting the objectors in one by one. This infuriated the objectors. The next morning they assembled nearby and then marched towards the inquiry room. The inspector ordered the doors locked, but the objectors heaved against them. David Mole and the Deputy Treasury Solicitor tried with others to keep them closed, but eventually failed. The inspector adjourned and subsequently the project was abandoned.

South Woodham Ferrers is an area lying close to the River Crouch in Essex. In the 1970s much of it consisted of plot lands, small rural plots of land sold during the 1920s and 1930s to people who built weekend cottages and shacks on them and in some cases cultivated smallholdings on them. They could be scruffy and unattractive, though sometimes as I saw on a site visit they had a quiet, away-from-it-all charm. Much of the area was attractively tranquil, though I could see that it was neither urban nor truly rural. Essex County Council planned a small new town there, to incorporate such housing as existed and to provide additional housing needed there. I was briefed on the Council's behalf and the proposal duly succeeded at inquiry. The sizeable new town of South Woodham Ferrers is the result.

Winchester College, one of my clients on the M3 inquiry, brought me several cases. One of the most delightful concerned the Sydling Valley in Dorset, in that area which contained such evocative villages as Toller Porcorum and Piddletrenthide. The valley and its hillsides were farmland. Through the valley, from up on the downs near a hamlet appropriately called Up Sydling flowed Sydling Water, fed by springs from the underground aquifer, and passing through a small, attractive village called Sydling St Nicholas. The Wessex Water Company wanted to abstract millions of gallons of water to supply the growing town of Yeovil about twelve miles to the north. The College was one of the objectors, owning as it did some of the farmland.

This was the first and only case I did under the Water Acts, and fascinating it was. I had not realized on a casual visit how important the stream and the aquifer were to that valley, but the fact was that the farmland relied on pumping water from the ground, the stream was used for extensive watercress beds, and the attractiveness of the village was greatly dependent on an adequate flow of water in the stream. I learnt about the effects of large-scale water abstraction and cones of depression, and we successfully persuaded the inspector that the risks involved with the Water Company's project were too great. It remains a lovely valley.

In the course of all this work, I had managed to work out how one should go about cross-examining an expert witness, whether a highway engineer, planner, architect or any other consultant. The crucial thing is to plan the cross-examination, with the ultimate objective being to get the expert to agree to an important proposition. So one begins by identifying for oneself that proposition. Then one must think about how the witness would seek to avoid agreeing with the proposition if it was put to him straight out early in the cross-examination. Having identified his likely escape routes, one must block them before putting the vital question. I sometimes thought of it as blocking the exits from a rabbit warren before putting the ferret down. One had to achieve such blocking by getting the witness to agree early on to a number of apparently uncontroversial propositions.

I also observed there was a great variety of styles of advocacy at the Bar. Merely at planning inquiries, they ranged from the crisp, incisive and sometimes brutal style of Frank Layfield or Graham Eyre to, at the other end of the scale, the more traditional, slightly pompous approach of Sir Derek Walker-Smith. He was a charming, portly figure, somewhat red-faced, a former Conservative MP and Health Minister, who was once heard at an inquiry to rise to his feet and say words to this effect: 'Loath though I am, sir, to disrupt the even pace of these important, nay critical, proceedings, I feel that I ought to bring to your attention a matter which has been giving rise to concern amongst some of those present, even though it may not be something which has been observed by those of my learned friends who have been more involved in dealing with witnesses over the recent period ...' and so on for three or four minutes. Eventually it became clear that he was simply asking for a window to be opened because it was hot! However, what was remarkable was that, however full of subordinate clauses, however toweringly cumulative his sentences, they always managed to end up grammatically. That took some skill.

6

Family and Politics

*He knows nothing; and he thinks he knows everything. That
points clearly to a political career.*

GEORGE BERNARD SHAW

Through all this our family life went on. Gillian had stopped
working in order to look after the children. I had retained
my interest in politics, and began to look for a constituency
which I could fight on behalf of the Labour Party. Shirley
Williams encouraged several of us, some from the Young
Fabians, to try for her old seat of Hitchin, which was being
affected by redistribution. It was probably unwinnable in its
new form, but I could hope for nothing better for my first
election. In the event, the nomination went to a fellow barrister,
Ann Mallalieu.

In the end, I was selected as the prospective candidate for
Taunton, a seat held by Edward du Cann for the Tories. He had a
healthy majority, but I nursed it for some time and was greatly

impressed by the local Labour party. Several of its members became good friends of ours, and there was a complete absence of back-biting or in-fighting. It also meant that we came to know much of Somerset well, and did a lot of walking on the Quantocks and on Exmoor. The general election came in February 1974, with Edward Heath relying on the slogan 'Who Governs Britain?' Many friends and members of chambers came down to help, irrespective of their political views. In Taunton, du Cann unsurprisingly won, but we reduced his majority by a good amount and kept the Liberals well behind in third place. During the campaign our children had noticed that there were more posters in people's windows saying 'Du Cann' than saying 'Keene'. They decided that this was the result of too few posters being available, and so they set to and made their own. It was one of the last of the old-fashioned campaigns, with candidates addressing meetings in village halls and elsewhere, sometimes three or four meetings an evening.

It was likely that there would be another election soon, since Harold Wilson, though successful, had only a narrow majority. I thought it sensible to try to find a winnable seat for next time. I had not succeeded by the time an election was called and so agreed to stand in Croydon South, one of the safest Conservative seats in the country. We duly lost.

A little while later Gilly and I decided to move from Blackheath to north of the river. She had always admired the Hampstead area and so we started searching in the hot, very dry summer of 1976. House prices had been falling and we found ourselves able to afford a detached house in Belsize Park. Contracts were duly exchanged, and on the date for completion we began the two-day job of seeing our furniture, clothes and household goods loaded into removal vehicles. At that point we heard from our solicitors that the vendor's solicitors had just told them that he could not complete that day. It was unclear why. In the end we decided that it was best to carry out the second day's removal and complete our own sale to our purchasers. This we did.

There then ensued a long and fraught delay. It turned out that our Belsize Park vendor was in negative equity and was trying to persuade the finance company who held his mortgage to waive the balance between what he owed them and what he was getting from us. The finance company was unpersuaded. The result was that we and our two children were literally homeless for about six weeks, which we spent lodging with Gillian's parents, with Konrad and Lisl Schiemann and by taking a holiday. Eventually completion took place, though we never gathered how the problem was resolved. I then decided to sue the vendor for his failure to complete in time, thereby breaching his contract. My solicitor doubted whether we were entitled to damages, but I disagreed. The vendor paid up, and years later the courts took the same view as I had done of the availability of damages.

The move to Belsize Park proved a real success. The schools were better, the journey to work was easier, and Hampstead Heath was nearby. We also made new friends. Edward became a close friend of Giles Coren, the son of Anne and Alan Coren, and we found that we got on very well with them. Giles and his sister Victoria were much the same age as our two children, and we started spending many weekends together.

The two families also joined together for holidays in a villa in the South of France and in the Algarve for a couple of years. Alan at that time was deputy editor and soon to be editor of the humorous magazine *Punch*. He was very amusing company. I remember him walking back through a garden centre, declaring 'I have seen the fuchsia – and it works!' He had got a First in English at Oxford, and his literary knowledge shone through his humour. He was, of course, not wise-cracking all the time, but in the presence of someone new, a form of fresh audience, it was like pressing a button – the humour came fast and furious. On one occasion in the south of France, I remember him referring to cicadas as 'reverse watchdogs' – when someone approached the house, they stopped their noise! His books are mostly collections of his articles from *Punch* and *The Times* and most are still hilarious today – James Bond as a geriatric secret agent, for example. Even the titles of some of his columns were eye-catching. One, based (as so often they were) on a newspaper cutting, this one about the discovery that Beethoven's liver showed he was a heavy drinker, was headed 'Go Easy, Mr Beethoven, that was your fifth'. He also wrote a series of children's books about a boy called Arthur, one of which he generously dedicated to Harriet and Edward. Anne was a consultant anaesthetist, bright, hugely likeable and very entertaining, and they were both bridge fanatics. They tried to teach us, but in vain. Even though Alan died far too young in 2007, the family ties remain. Giles was Edward's best man at his wedding, and is godfather to Edward's oldest child Olivia. His speech at Edward's wedding, which took place in the United States, was outstandingly witty and had several of the older women present wanting to take him home with them.

Harriet was by the late 1970s at Gillian's old school, North London Collegiate, which turned out to be a much more conservative and rigid place than in her time there. Understandably Harriet tended to react against this. Edward went from the Hall School in Belsize Park to Westminster, winning the second scholarship and becoming a weekly boarder. Neither Gillian nor I had been particularly enthusiastic about boarding schools, but since I was often away at inquiries during the week, a regime where he came home at weekends seemed acceptable. We were, of course, all together in the holidays. One of those was particularly memorable: an overland trip to Greece. This came about in unusual circumstances. I had done a lot of work during the Roskill inquiry on airport safety and knew that the (then) Athens airport had a steeper than usual approach path. Gillian had been involved professionally in an incident at Athens airport concerning a Swiss Airline plane and had not been impressed by how the incident had been tackled. So, though we wanted to take the kids to Greece, neither of us wanted to fly there. The result was a delightful trip by boat and train: to Paris by ferry and train; then an overnight sleeper to Venice, waking up just before arrival and walking down the station steps to the Grand Canal and its vaporettos; after a few days there, trains down the length of Italy to Bari, followed by ferry to Corfu. There we spent several days before crossing to the Greek mainland by ferry to Patras, after which we explored some of the Peloponnese as well as the island of Naxos. Perhaps irrationally we were willing to fly back from Athens to the UK and undoubtedly it cost us more than conventional return air fares, but it was a fascinating and very enjoyable experience.

We didn't see much of my brother Andrew, partly because we were very busy but partly because we had drifted apart. He chose not to go to university but to go into railway management. He had always been a great train enthusiast since boyhood, and from time to time when we were both very young our mother had been persuaded to take us up to near Clapham Junction to watch the Golden Arrow train to Paris go past. So a job in the railways, first with British Rail and then with the successor private rail companies, suited him very well. But our interests and our political views had diverged, and when we met, sad to say, we found that we had little in common.

I had put thoughts of a political career on a back-burner while I established my planning practice, and I was also becoming concerned about the increasing influence of the far left within the Labour Party. As a result I didn't stand in the 1979 election. When the Party Conference adopted unilateral nuclear disarmament and exit from the European Community and when in 1980 Michael Foot was elected leader, I decided that I could no longer support the party. I welcomed the breakaway to form the Social Democratic Party, although I could see how difficult it would be for a third party to make real headway in British politics. As it happened, we were in for many years of Conservative government.

Gillian was in a position by now to return to work, but academic posts were in very short supply. After discussion, she decided to read for the Bar, which she did, and was in due course taken on by Fountain Court chambers. It turned out not to be a great success. It should have been, since her clear mind and ability as an advocate should have brought her lots of work, but she discovered eventually that one of the most senior members of chambers thought that she was not serious about her legal career and that she was in it merely for pin-money. That, coupled with some out-dated anti-female attitudes amongst some of the clerks, proved a real handicap. When those chambers started concentrating more on commercial work than the general common law and personal injury work that she enjoyed, she decided to move. She joined chambers at Farrer's Building, where she felt much more welcome.

7

Into Silk

We are all Adam's children, but silk makes the difference.

THOMAS FULLER

I had had no serious thoughts about becoming a QC until Douglas Frank, still head of our chambers, encouraged me to do so in December 1979. I had to rush around to get the necessary material together and just got the application in before the deadline. We were staying in a gîte in rural France over the following Easter when the farmer's wife came running down the path from the farmhouse, calling 'Monsieur, monsieur, téléphone!' It was my clerk, Leslie Page, to tell me that I had got silk, as had Konrad Schiemann. Leslie could see that this was a big boost for chambers, getting two silks in one year, and indeed it was after that that the chambers really began to expand until it became one of the leading planning sets in the country, now based at 4 and 5, Gray's Inn Square.

My work now improved in size and quality. I no longer needed a silk to lead me even in big inquiries. I was immediately launched into another Third London Airport inquiry, this time into a proposal by the British Airports Authority to locate it at . . . where else but Stansted! After all, the BAA owned it. I was retained by Essex, Hertfordshire and Cambridgeshire County Councils, several district councils and Cambridge University to oppose it. I had two excellent junior counsel, Duncan Ouseley, later a High Court judge, and John Steel, later a QC, and a first-rate instructing solicitor, Robert Jameson.

We needed this talent. The BAA instructed Lionel Reed QC, a very experienced planning silk possessed of great skills. He was a formidable opponent. The inquiry inspector was another experienced planning silk, Graham Eyre QC. He was no doubt concerned to get the inquiry concluded as quickly as possible, and to that end he worked himself and all the parties very hard. All evidence in chief was taken as read, and we moved rapidly from one witness to the next. He probably worked himself too hard, in that he was subsequently never the brilliant advocate that he had been before that inquiry. He understood that he had been promised at least a knighthood and probably a seat on the bench if he took on this difficult inquiry at financial rates far below his normal level, and he was subsequently bitter that he was never appointed a judge and that the knighthood was delayed for five years after the end of the inquiry.

We probably made his task worse and certainly lengthened the inquiry. In conjunction with British Airways we were suggesting that a preferable alternative to Stansted would be a fifth terminal at Heathrow. But the BAA were stressing the urgency of getting the new airport capacity available, and we could see that the delay in producing a further planning application for a fifth terminal and yet another public inquiry into it would be a powerful argument against such an alternative. I was well aware that one did not need to own a piece of land in order to submit a planning application for its development. All that was necessary was to notify the landowner. So I advised and we decided to put in a planning application for a fifth terminal at Heathrow on the then sludge works, where Terminal 5 in fact now stands. It was done in the name of one of my clients, Uttlesford District Council in Essex, and as we had anticipated the Secretary of State for the Environment had no alternative but to 'call in' the application for his own decision and to refer it to Graham Eyre's inquiry. So the Stansted Airport inquiry became a two-stage affair, first at Quendon Hall near Stansted and then at Heathrow itself.

In opposition to Stansted, we particularly emphasized the impact that the airport would have on the attractive towns, villages and countryside in that area, because of the urban development that it would bring. Major airports generate a lot of jobs, directly and indirectly, and that in turn means offices, warehouses, some factories and a great deal of new housing. Nor was it an area that needed job creation.

As is evident, we did not win. We did, however, achieve a couple of useful results. Graham Eyre came out emphatically against there ever being a second runway at Stansted, calling it 'an environmental catastrophe', and he recommended that, after the current Stansted scheme, the fifth terminal at Heathrow should be favourably considered.

I had more success with airports when I was briefed to promote the development of a completely new airport in the London docklands. Most of the docks there were no longer functioning. The Upper Docks on the Thames had fallen into disuse because of containerisation and the move to roll-on/roll-off cargo ships, with the traffic moving more and more downstream to Tilbury and indeed away from the Thames altogether to places like Felixstowe. My clients were the construction company Mowlem and the proposal was for an airport located in the old Royal Docks, from where the last ship had left in 1982. The airport was planned to use the Royal Albert dock and the King George V dock together with the quay which lay between them. My first site visit revealed a sad picture of dereliction. The quay, later to become the runway, was crowded with rusting cranes and gantries, the windows in the sheds and other buildings were broken, there was dirt and rubbish everywhere, and the surrounding area was clearly in need of some form of economic uplift.

The planning application was for a 'Stolport', a short take-off and landing airport, using principally Dash 7 aircraft made by De Havilland. This was a turbo-prop aircraft with a remarkable ability to utilize short runways, which since the Royal Docks quay was only just over 3,500 feet long was a vital characteristic. A public inquiry in 1983 lasted over sixty working days, with opposition coming from the Greater London Council and some local people. It was objected that, however quiet aircraft like the Dash 7 were, it would become much noisier if jets were used. We pointed out that jets could be prohibited by a condition on any planning permission, and if the operators wanted at some future date to introduce jets, there would have to be a fresh planning permission and almost certainly a new public inquiry. One novel argument raised was that the proposed airport might well fail, leaving an empty site. We responded with two points: first, it was unlikely to fail, and we produced forecasts to demonstrate this; secondly, the fact that a proposed development might not be commercially successful was not a valid objection in planning law.

In the event the inspector recommended approval and the Secretary of State in due course granted permission. The airport opened in 1987; it has grown since its early days and, as London City Airport, now deals with over four-and-a-half million passengers a year. I would be falsely modest if I pretended other than it was the achievement of which I was most proud.

One incident from that case still remains fresh in my mind. In preparing for the inquiry, my clients suggested that I might like to take a flight in a STOL aircraft. Such planes were, it seemed, flying regularly from Heathrow to Cornwall, operated by Brymon Airways who were supporters of the docklands project. This sounded fun, and so I agreed. I tipped up at Heathrow early one morning and off we went. All went well, and then towards the end of the flight I was asked if I would like to come up into the cockpit to see the landing. I got up and sat next to the pilot, and he started to descend.

Looking back, I realize that gradients, even on roads, can be exaggerated when one is some distance away. In the Dash 7, we seemed to be coming into land at a horrifically steep angle. I suddenly wondered if the pilot had miscalculated and we were going to hit the runway with a crash. Promising career cut short. As is evident from my writing this account, the pilot knew perfectly well what he was doing and we landed entirely safely.

By now I was regularly appearing on behalf of developers to achieve planning permissions. The reality of the Planning Bar was (and probably still is) that, in your junior days when your fees are relatively low, you are briefed to act on behalf of public bodies, usually district councils or boroughs as the local planning authority. The public sector was and is strapped for cash and often could not afford the higher fees of QCs and the most experienced juniors. It is the private sector, principally the developers, who can afford to retain the more expensive and more experienced members of the Bar. Hence the frequent sight of a QC appearing at a planning inquiry for the developers, opposed by junior counsel for the local planning authority. Planning inspectors are usually well aware of this inequality of experience and generally try to make some allowance for it.

New large shopping developments also featured largely in my practice. One was Bluewater Park, near Dartford in Kent. It was located in the Green Belt, where a major shopping development would not normally be contemplated. But our proposal was to site it in a very large disused chalk pit, with the sides 50m high, so that the buildings would be below the surrounding ground level and have no real impact on the surrounding area or the efficacy of the Green Belt. Chris Patten as Secretary of State accepted this and granted permission in 1990. It was the largest retail and leisure centre in Europe when it opened nine years later.

This was just after the Trafford Centre in Manchester, another very large retail and leisure development. This involved two major public inquiries because of issues over the impact on traffic on the M60 motorway. We managed to persuade the inspector that such problems were soluble and permission was eventually granted. Some objectors challenged the grant of permission in the courts and the case went up all the way to the House of Lords Judicial Committee where the permission was upheld.

Sometimes at inquiries one was presented by one's opponents with a forensic gift. Such happened at Doncaster, where I was opposing a toxic waste incinerator on behalf of the local authority. Lionel Read QC acted for the developer, leading Rhodri Price Lewis. I knew them both well. One vital issue was whether the operating company would be able to take sufficient precautions to ensure that no toxic material escaped into the air of this largely residential neighbourhood or into the ground, which was important as a water source. We were all assured that the company's experience showed that all would be well – any toxins would be burnt off in the very high temperatures. Then the company's senior director mentioned in evidence that at one of their existing incinerators elsewhere, a detailed daily log was kept. 'Is there any reason', I asked him, 'why this inquiry should not be provided with copies of those logs?' I could see Lionel and Rhodri stiffen. 'No, none at all,' came the answer.

It was a godsend. The daily logs were full of complaints by the individual staff about temperature failures, and inadequate controls by the previous shift. 'Plume horrible, everything horrible' ran one entry. We produced a short edited version for the planning inspector, which made for vivid reading. The ultimate decision rejected the incinerator, and Rhodri still flinches when I tease him about it.

Late on in my time at the Bar I had the unusual experience of dealing with a proposal to dig a new deep coal mine, in this case between Coventry and Birmingham. This was unusual because mining generally was in marked decline, but British Coal saw some potential near Berkswell. This, however, fell within a very narrow part of the Green Belt and a very important one, separating Coventry and Birmingham, as my clients, Solihull Borough Council, emphasized. Eventually we won. It was another case demonstrating the variety of work which one had at the Planning Bar.

I found myself acting as an independent planning inspector at one stage in the 1980s. This arose from the conflict between the Greater London Council under Ken Livingstone and the then Prime Minister, Margaret Thatcher. She abolished the GLC in 1986, but the issue then arose of what to do with County Hall, in part a Grade II listed building originally the home of the old London County Council and then of the GLC. It still contained the headquarters of the Inner London Education Authority (ILEA) and the Fire Services Authority, but it was now owned by the London Residuary Body.

Planning applications were put in for a variety of uses, mostly hotel and offices, and I conducted a public inquiry. In the end I concluded that the main building should be retained for London government uses, such as the ILEA and the Fire Services for which it was especially suited, but that the more modern north and south blocks could be devoted to other uses. I was aware that this recommendation might not be palatable to the government, and so it proved. The Secretary of State, Nicholas Ridley, refused to accept my recommendation. His decision was in due course challenged in the courts, but ultimately without success.

Interspersed with these planning inquiries was some commercial work and a lengthy arbitration at the International Chamber of Commerce in Paris. That resulted from a disaster in 1977 in Qatar in the Gulf where a natural gas complex designed by Shell, who also supervised its construction, caught fire and exploded, killing seven people and causing immense damage. The complex was owned by Qatar's nationalized petro-chemical industry, which claimed a huge sum in damages against Shell. Mark Littman QC and I were retained to act for Shell, he to handle the legal issues, I the technical ones. Shell were wonderful clients for whom to work: they found high quality expert witnesses, who outside the hearing gave me one-to-one tuition on physics, engineering, welding techniques and similar subjects of which I had known little if anything. The hearing in 1984 lasted for six working months spread over a year, and I was accommodated in the Grand Hotel near the old Opéra in the winter time and in an apartment on the Champs Elysées in the summer. Mark managed with a couple of suites at the Ritz! We were successful in our defence of Shell, and I got to know the lovely city of Paris better than any other than London.

Inevitably, not all my inquiries resulted in success. Thus I failed to get permission for a new business park at Brooklands

PLATE 1 *Mother, brother Andrew (on chair) and me.*

PLATE 2 *Father.*

PLATE 3 *On holiday in Dovercourt, about 1947.*

LABOUR GAIN COUNCIL SEAT

54 MAJORITY IN THREE-CORNERED FIGHT

The Socialists, who, at the beginning of the year had only one councillor on Twickenham Corporation, brought their total representation to four in Thursday's by-election in the Hampton Hill ward. Their candidate, Mr. Geoffrey J. Samuel, a schoolteacher, of 28, Lebanon Court, Twickenham, was elected with a majority of 54 votes in a three-cornered contest.

This is the first time since 1949 that Hampton Hill has had a Socialist councillor.

The by-election was caused by the appointment of the former Conservative councillor, Mr. M. W. Garrett, as an alderman.

On Thursday, 3,081 of the 7,498

Minister presents school prizes

The Minister of Education (Mr. Geoffrey Lloyd) presented the prizes at Hampton Grammar School speech day on Thursday last week. In the picture on the right he is seen with the Headmaster (Mr. G. J. N. Whitfield).

PLATE 4 *G. J. N. Whitfield (left), Headmaster of Hampton Grammar School.*

PLATE 5 *Balliol College, Oxford.*

```
CENtral 1878/9.                    2 Crown Office Row,

                                        Temple, E.C.4.

                 Fees of.

                        MR. DAVID KEENE
```

1965

		CITY OF OXFORD DEVELOPMENT PLAN OBJECTION NO.40. BALLIOL COLLEGE, OXFORD.			
Jan	20	Refresher	5	10	0
"	21	Refresher	5	10	0
"	22	Refresher	5	10	0
"	26	Refresher	5	10	0
"	27	Refresher	5	10	0
"	28	Refresher	5	10	0
"	29	Refresher	5	10	0
Feb	2	Refresher	5	10	0
			44	0	0

```
Messrs. Henry G. Galpin and Co.,
Solicitors,
Oxford.                          LL
```

PLATE 6 *First fee note as barrister, 1965.*

PLATE 7 *October 1974 election leaflet.*

PLATE 8 *October 1974 election leaflet.*

PLATE 9 *Early family life, with Harriet and Edward.*

PLATE 10 *Gillian, Call to the Bar 1980.* © *Universal Pictorial Press and Agency Ltd.*

PLATE 11 *Mother and father in retirement.*

PLATE 12 *The site of South Woodham Ferrers town.*

PLATE 13 *London City Airport © Getty/W-F Xue.*

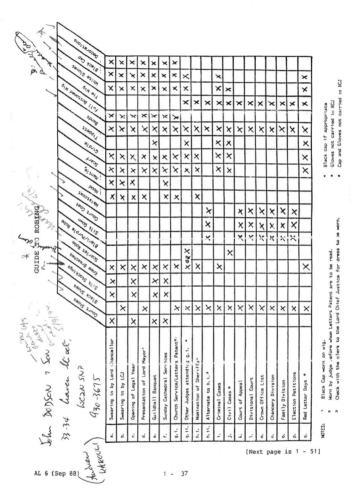

PLATE 14 *Matrix for High Court judges' robes for each occasion.*

David Morris and Helen Steel outside the High Court in London yesterday after the result of their appeal

McDonald's pair win partial victory

By Terence Shaw, Legal Correspondent

TWO penniless campaigners, who were ordered to pay McDonald's £60,000 libel damages two years ago after losing what became the longest trial in English legal history, won a partial victory in the Appeal Court yesterday.

Three appeal judges dismissed the majority of grounds on which David Morris, 44, a former postman, and Helen Steel, 33, a bar worker, had sought to challenge the judgment of Mr Justice Bell after a 314-day trial that they had libelled the fast food chain.

But Lord Justice Pill, who was sitting with Lord Justice May and Mr Justice Keene, upheld some of the grounds of their appeal and reduced the damages that the couple must pay to McDonald's from £60,000 to £40,000.

After a trial spread over two and a half years in which the couple defended themselves and which has been estimated to have cost McDonald's £10 million, Mr Justice Bell ruled that the company had been libelled by most of the allegations in a London Greenpeace campaign leaflet entitled: *What's Wrong With McDonald's*.

But he also ruled that the pamphlet had been justified in claiming that the fast food chain exploited children in its advertising, was cruel to some of the animals used in its products and that its restaurants paid low wages to British workers.

In their 309-page judgment, handed down yesterday, the three appeal judges said it was fair comment for the appellants to say McDonald's workers worldwide "do badly in terms of pay and conditions".

They also said the allegation that "if one eats enough McDonald's food, one's diet may well become high in fat, etc, with the very real risk of heart disease" was justified.

But they agreed with the judge that many of the charges in the leaflet had not been shown to be justified.

Outside the court, Miss Steel said: "There should be protection for the right to criticise rich and powerful organisations that have an immense effect on people's lives."

She said they intended to seek leave to appeal to the House of Lords and, if necessary, they would be taking the case to the European Court of Human Rights "to protect the public's right to criticise multinational companies".

PLATE 15 *Macdonald libel case* © *Telegraph Media Group Ltd*

PLATE 16 *The house at St Martin d'Oydes, France.*

PLATE 17 *The village of St Martin d'Oydes (house in centre foreground).*

PLATE 18 *Walking with the Blairs in France, early 1990s.*

PLATE 19 *Tony Blair and Lionel Jospin meet as PMs at the house.*

PLATE 20 *On appointment to Court of Appeal, with Gillian and Harriet.*

near Weybridge, largely because it was in the green belt. It was nonetheless fascinating to drive on the old race-track, and to see the photos of past racing drivers in the clubhouse, including one of a youthful Barbara Cartland, the romantic novelist, in helmet and racing gear. Another failure was attempting to get permission for an expansion of Pinewood Film Studios near Iver Heath in Buckinghamshire. That too was rejected on Green Belt grounds. But on the whole my practice seemed to be going well, and in 1993 I was elected Vice-Chairman of the Planning Bar, and Chairman the following year.

Some years earlier I had been advised that I should apply to become an Assistant Recorder (that is, a part-time judge, usually in criminal cases). I was accepted in 1986 and the appointment was, in effect, confirmed three years later when I was made a Recorder. Such part-timers are expected to sit as judges at least twenty days a year. It meant that I was presiding over criminal trials with a jury, a forum of which I had no previous experience whatever, but I was sent on a first-rate training session and then did a two-week judicial pupillage with the Resident Judge at Southwark Crown Court, Gerald Butler QC. He was full of kindness and patience and, having come from a non-criminal law practice himself, he could well appreciate my abysmal lack of knowledge. I took copious notes. Nonetheless, it was an anxious moment when I addressed my first jury, not from the Bar but from the bench. I formed the view that Crown Court Recorders have a particularly difficult job to do when it comes to sentencing an offender. The offence will often be below the level of seriousness where it automatically attracts a prison sentence. So the judge has to decide whether this is a case for a custodial or a non-custodial sentence, and that is often far from easy. Certainly it is more of a problem than deciding on the precise number of years' imprisonment to impose, because even a short custodial sentence is going to have significant consequences for most offenders.

Meanwhile, much had been happening in my personal and family life. My father died suddenly and unexpectedly in August 1987. I was very sad that I had not seen him in his final few days, but it was not thought that his illness was serious. Our daughter Harriet was in the USA at the time. She had left school uncertain as to whether she wanted to go to university, but eventually she accepted a place at Sussex University, where she read English in the School of English and American Studies. She emerged with a good degree, followed by a teaching diploma in London. After spending some time as a volunteer in Tanzania building clinics and health centres, she moved into primary school teaching in London. That was a role for which she was well suited. As she said to us, she wasn't afraid of the naughty children – having been one herself, she could handle them.

Edward decided that he wanted to read PPE at Oxford. He visited various colleges on their open days, and eventually chose Balliol – not from any paternal pressure, which would have been fatal. I was nonetheless delighted. His offer of a place there came initially in a phone call before he had had any sort of an interview. He was worried that this was a hoax being performed by one of his friends, and initially it seemed that he might have grounds for scepticism. We contacted several academic friends in Oxford, who all said that they had never heard of a place being offered without an interview. In the end, I got in touch with one of my Balliol contemporaries, John Jones, who was now the Dean there, and he agreed to investigate. He came back to say that offer was genuine. Apparently the college had had three applicants for PPE who were so obviously acceptable that it was decided to take them with no interview. It was, as events showed, an outstanding year for Balliol's PPE admissions. Three years later the college achieved its highest ever number of PPE firsts. Edward went on to do a Master's degree in International Relations and then a Doctorate, both at the LSE, where he met Molly Cochran. She was a highly intelligent, attractive young woman originating from Athens, Georgia. They fell for each other and were married on St Simon's Island, just off the Georgia coast.

OUT OF THE ARENA

8

The Bench Full-Time

*I could have been a judge, but I never had the
Latin for the judging.*

PETER COOK in 'Beyond the Fringe'

I found that I enjoyed the new challenges of sitting as a part-time judge. It was a huge change from my planning practice, and of course it meant a lot of responsibility for making decisions instead of trying to persuade someone else how an issue should be decided. I still greatly enjoyed advocacy, and the thrill of a successful cross-examination or speech remained fresh. Even so, I was a little surprised when, in December 1993, I bumped into Tom Bingham, at that time Master of the Rolls and so head of the civil division of the Court of Appeal, at a social event and I mentioned the topic of the bench. He said to me: 'I gather, David, that you don't want to go onto the bench.' I was taken aback and replied: 'Wherever did you get that idea?' 'Ah', he said, 'so would you be interested?' I made it clear that I would. Those were the days when one did not and, I think, could not apply to become a High Court judge, and so that conversation was fortuitous.

Six months later, I was in the middle of promoting a second runway for Manchester Airport. It was a proposal which I had been living with for some time, for my clients, a group consisting of Manchester City Council and other Manchester local authorities, had come to me to discuss the best location for the new runway, reconciling the need to maximize its capacity with minimizing environmental impact, before putting in a planning application. That early consultation was unusual but obviously sensible, especially as there was an attractive wooded valley close to where the runway would ideally have been sited.

The inquiry had been running for some months when I got a message at my hotel to ring the Lord Chancellor's Department. On doing so, I was asked to come to see him early the next week, this being a Friday. I agreed. Gillian had come up to Manchester so that we could spent part of that weekend walking in the Peak District. We walked, but I don't think we took in much of the scenery. We were too busy thinking over what the message might be. We were tolerably sure that I was going to be offered some sort of appointment, but what? Being at the peak of my career as a planning silk, I was most reluctant to accept an appointment below the level of the High Court, such as a circuit judge or a member of the Lands Tribunal. But I was far from confident that it was the High Court that was in the Lord Chancellor's mind.

However, it was. James Mackay, the Lord Chancellor, was charming and friendly, as I have subsequently always found him to be. I indicated that I wanted to accept, but that there was the problem of the Manchester Airport inquiry. I asked if I could postpone the appointment for six months. He wasn't very reassuring: 'The Lord Chief Justice needs someone now. What's more, you must bear in mind that we are about to change the retirement age for judges. If you leave it too long, you'll have to retire at 70, but if you come now, you can go on until you are 75!' All this in his soft Scottish accent. I didn't find the prospective change in retirement age very troubling, as I had always thought that there was much more to life than the law, but I also didn't want to risk the offer not being repeated. So I asked for a brief interval so as to be able to consult my Manchester clients.

They were kindness itself. It helped that I had an excellent number two at the inquiry, Andrew Gilbart QC, later Recorder of Manchester and then a High Court judge. Andrew was not a natural second fiddle, as he would readily admit, and I think that he was only too pleased to be able to take the lead. The clients knew that they would be in good hands, and they generously accepted that I should depart the inquiry. I later paid back part of my brief fee, which seemed only fair.

And so I became a High Court judge, assigned to the Queen's Bench Division which deals with most matters other than family and chancery work. Before I could be sworn in, I had to obtain the necessary judicial robes. I was amazed to find that, at that time, this required five different outfits: two for when sitting in criminal cases (one winter, one summer – the first using red wool with ermine trimmings, the second of red cotton and silk trimmings); two for civil trials (black, but otherwise similar to the criminal ones); and one plain black for use in the Administrative Court and the Court of Appeal's Criminal Division (the 'CACD'). How does a new judge get hold of these? Well, the classic way is through the Lord Chief Justice's clerk, who runs (or certainly ran) a form of second-hand robes mart. He took me through what was available and I picked ones which broadly-speaking fitted.

They did need either repair or cleaning or both. As for repair, I was directed to a little hole-in-the-wall establishment down a street near Charing Cross station. The manager treated this as an everyday occurrence. The only snag arose when it came to repairing a moth-eaten piece of ermine. He sucked his teeth and shook his head: 'Very difficult, sir. Wrong time of the year for ermine.' Somehow he managed.

As for cleaning, I was troubled. Between being told you're being appointed and being sworn in, the information as to your appointment is supposed to be kept secret. That is understandable, because you are still at the Bar and can appear in court, where you might have an unfair advantage if the secret was out. How then could I get the robes cleaned? I was told to take them to

Sketchleys on High Holborn – they were used to it. To achieve some small degree of discretion, Gillian took the robes there in a large bag, emptied them out, and the man behind the counter didn't turn a hair.

So complex were the sartorial combinations for different occasions and courts that High Court judges were issued with a chart, in matrix form, with nineteen occasions/courts down one axis and twenty items of robes and ancillary gear along the other.

So I was sworn in as a judge in October 1994 in the Lord Chief Justice's Court and went straightaway out on circuit to sit at Winchester. Queen's Bench judges normally spent half of each legal term sitting in London and half out on circuit. There is a degree of choice as to which Crown Court on circuit one goes to, but one's position in the choosing process moves around from term to term so that everybody gets a fair turn. I was very fortunate as Winchester was always regarded as a prized location.

Indeed it was. The judges' lodgings there were not only pleasant but located in the cathedral precinct, so that in the mornings before court one could often hear the choirboys practising. If heaven could be, as Sydney Smith suggested, eating foie gras to the sound of trumpets, lying in bed in the morning at Winchester listening to the Cathedral choir rehearsing must run it a close second. There was one other High Court judge in the lodgings at the same time, Tom Morison, whom I knew fairly well. As the senior judge, he had the right to decide whether we should dress for dinner in black tie, a practice rapidly going out of fashion but still insisted on by one or two senior judges. Tom fortunately was all for casual wear. I found myself spending my six weeks at Winchester trying not very difficult murder cases, a gentle introduction to serious crime.

I had been assigned a clerk by now, Trevor, who accompanied me both on circuit and in London. He was very experienced, if a little gloomy at times. He made sure that I was properly robed at all times, including one aspect that was really bizarre. When sitting in crime, a High Court judge carries into court each day a black cap and a pair of white kid gloves, both relics of the time when this country retained capital punishment. The black cap was, of course, worn in the past when a judge had to pass a sentence of execution on an offender. It consists of a woollen rectangle of black material which would perch on top of the judge's wig. These days it simply sits in front of the judge on the bench. It did occasionally occur to me to wonder what would happen if a judge these days were to put it on when passing sentence, a mischievous thought which I never took seriously. The white gloves were apparently put on if a judge in those long-past times came to the end of an assize without having sentenced anyone to death – a Maiden Assize. Like the black cap, it is irrelevant these days. Moreover, most of the judges I know would quit the bench if capital punishment were ever to be reintroduced.

Back in London that first term I found myself sitting with the Lord Chief Justice and Mr Justice Mantell in the Court of Appeal Criminal Division. No doubt this was a deliberate way of providing guidance to new High Court judges. Though the Criminal Division forms part of the Court of Appeal, a criminal case that comes up on appeal is heard not by three Lord Justices of Appeal (as happens in the Civil Division) but by one Lord Justice of Appeal and either two High Court Judges as 'wingers' or one High Court Judge and an experienced Circuit Judge. The Circuit judiciary forms the level just below the High Court in the hierarchy. In either division of the Court of Appeal, the practice is for the three judges to meet before the day's cases start, so as to discuss their views of the cases. On the first day of my week in the CACD with the Lord Chief Justice, Peter Taylor, we finished our discussion with five or ten minutes to spare. Peter and Charles Mantell then turned to discussing the benefits of a prostate operation! I thought to myself that I really had moved into the realms of the elderly.

When in London my time was divided between the CACD, the Administrative Court (dealing with judicial review of decisions by public bodies) and the Employment Appeal Tribunal. Out on circuit, judicial life seemed less pressured, mainly because cases could only proceed as fast as a jury could absorb the evidence put before them. The criminal trials on circuit seemed mainly to consist of murder or rape cases, though

I did have one horrendous historic sexual abuse case in Reading with multiple victims.

In the middle of my first term I had to go to Buckingham Palace to be knighted. This was automatic on appointment to the High Court bench, as was made clear to one colleague who tried to decline it. I was met at a door to the palace by an equerry in military uniform who was taking me along a thickly carpeted corridor to the Queen. After a few yards, however, he asked me to slow down, telling me that he couldn't walk very fast in these – and pointing downwards. At that moment I realized that he was wearing spurs – not ideal for walking on carpets. The investiture at that time for High Court judges involved an entirely private audience with the Queen. I emerged duly knighted.

Judges in court do not wear the full-length wigs popularly depicted in cartoons. We wear short wigs, and even these have been dispensed with in civil cases. Not so in criminal cases, because they are thought to confer a welcome degree of anonymity. I had some evidence of this while sitting in Lewes. One day my list of cases finished early and so, as judges were encouraged to do, I arranged to visit the local prison that afternoon. The Deputy Governor of Lewes Prison took me around, and as we entered an internal yard from one corner, a prisoner and prison officer came in from the opposite corner. I recognized the prisoner as someone who had been convicted before me only a week or two earlier of murder, and I had sentenced him to life imprisonment. He looked at me with an air of puzzlement. He obviously thought that he had seen me before somewhere, but could not work out where. After a little while, the penny dropped and a broad smile spread across his face. But the fact that I was no longer wearing a wig had greatly delayed his recognition of me. He afterwards wrote me a number of letters, complaining that his conviction had been a miscarriage of justice.

There are those who question the value of juries in criminal trials. My own experience suggests that they provide the most reliable method of assessing guilt or innocence. I was always relieved that it was the jury which had to decide who they believed, who was telling the truth. A judge from a legal background has no extra insight into this difficult task. Moreover, I found that juries generally approached their job with great responsibility. In trials with a complex combination of several defendants and a number of separate charges, the jury would invariably return verdicts which distinguished both between defendants and between offences. They did not usually just convict or acquit on the whole package, unless of course the prosecution's case stood or fell as a single entity. Sometimes they operate a sort of rough justice. One case I tried concerned an allegation of marital rape, where the evidence to my mind that the wife had not consented to having sex with her husband on this occasion was pretty strong. However, in evidence it also emerged that the wife had been having an affair around this time, and the jury acquitted the husband. It seemed to me that they were reluctant to see him imprisoned, as is usually inevitable in rape cases, in the circumstances surrounding this marriage.

Judges' lodgings get criticized as an unnecessary luxury. That is fair if one is dealing with lodgings serving one modest-sized Crown Court which may see a single High Court judge for half of each term. That is not efficient. Equally there were in my time lodgings serving courts within easy daily commute from London, places like Chelmsford or Reading. Those have been steadily closed. However, lodgings serving the bigger cities make more sense. If one is having to accommodate two, three or four judges, plus their clerks, with the necessary working rooms and security, it is economic to use lodgings rather than, say, hotels. Places like Birmingham, Manchester and Leeds are best served by premises devoted to accommodating a number of judges.

Of course, some of the smaller lodgings have, or had, charm, occasionally provided by the staff. Stafford was one such. The judges' lodgings there directly adjoined the old courthouse, and the judge could proceed from the lodgings to his or her seat on the bench without emerging into any public gaze on the way. Rumour had it that one judge, waking far later than he should, simply put on his robes over his pyjamas and marched into court. Stafford lodgings had no resident staff. When I sat there, we had to bring in someone, an 'itinerant butler'. He turned out to be a splendid relic of past ages. Sidney invariably wore a black tail coat at any time of day, wore white gloves to serve me breakfast and was taken aback that I was not going to dress for dinner in black tie. So far as I was concerned, I was there on my own and would wear what I liked in the evening. However, when for the first-time Gillian was coming to stay, Sidney's enthusiasm for formality returned. 'Shall I put out your Lordship's dinner jacket for tonight, as Lady Keene is coming?' 'No Sidney, not even for Lady Keene am I going to put on a dinner jacket!' Sidney was a great enthusiast for the horses and would regale us with his stories of success and failure.

Birmingham lodgings were a marked contrast. A large, even grand, post-war house in Edgbaston, with a lovely and extensive garden, it had been used in the past by judges conducting IRA trials. It therefore had numerous security measures, including high metal gates worked electronically. One needed an electronic device to get in or out, and at times it felt a little like being in a prison. The judges would refer to going out as 'Going over the Wall'. The sense of confinement was not eased by the butler and his wife, who seemed to regard the judges as an unwelcome intrusion on their lives.

Generally, however, I enjoyed my time on circuit. I was very impressed by the Bar in the towns and cities outside the southeast, who seemed to me to work with efficiency and co-operation in the conduct of cases and to possess great integrity. In London,

I found myself doing many administrative law cases, including town planning ones. These were a bit of a comfort zone for me, except that the daily list of administrative cases was always densely packed and preparation time was scarcely allowed for. I did nonetheless manage to fit in being Chairman of one of the committees of the Judicial Studies Board, the body which provided training for judges. I was Chairman of the Equal Treatment Committee, concerned with the full range of diversity. We eventually produced a handbook for the guidance of judges on questions of race, gender, sexual orientation, disability and other issues. Unsurprisingly, it brought down the wrath of the *Daily Mail* upon my head – not for the last time.

One controversial case which came my way concerned a proposal by the *Mail on Sunday* to publish parts of a work by David Shayler about his time as an officer of MI5. The government apparently only heard on the Friday before publication that the newspaper would not allow the security services to vet the material in advance and so it sought an injunction, the hearing into which had to take place on the Saturday. I was the duty judge that weekend, and so I had to deal with it. Since it was well known that I was on friendly terms with Cherie and Tony Blair, this was hardly ideal, but there seemed no escape. Even so, when counsel for both sides gathered at our Belsize Park home on the Saturday morning, I checked with Geoffrey Robertson QC, acting for the *Mail on Sunday*, whether he had any objection to me dealing with the case. As I carefully noted, he did not.

In the event I decided that a temporary injunction for a few days should be granted, until a longer further hearing could take place in court. This would ensure that national security, particularly in respect of surveillance operations, would not be unnecessarily prejudiced. The *Mail on Sunday* the next day went to town on my decision. 'Gagged' read its front page headline, with three further pages inside devoted to it. Nor did Geoffrey Robertson's agreement that I should hear the Attorney-General's application stop subsequent insinuations by others that I should not have done. Shayler himself was later convicted of breaches of the Official Secrets Act and sentenced to six months' imprisonment.

During the time I sat in London, I came of course to know the Royal Courts of Justice (RCJ) very well. Indeed, like all High Court Judges at that time, I had my room there in that imposing neo-Gothic building located at the eastern end of the Strand. It is a building of which, as a young barrister, I had been critical. All those turrets and towers seemed in the 1960s and 1970s dreadfully old-fashioned. But in time its architectural style came to seem more attractive to me, and in particular I came to admire the ingenuity of the architect, George Street, who was selected after a competition in the 1870s. He had first to cope with a significant rise in the level of the land which formed the site, rising from the south to the north as one moves away from the River Thames. Thus the 'back door' to the complex, the Carey Street side, is one floor higher than the Strand entrance. But in addition he had to produce a design which would enable the judges, when going from their private rooms into court and onto the bench, to avoid crossing the paths of and coming into contact with the parties to the case, counsel, solicitors and witnesses. Street solved this problem brilliantly. His design uses the concept of concentric circles around a central hall. The judges' rooms form an outer circle, with a corridor just inside. That corridor leads to the judges' entrances to the individual court rooms, which form the next inward circle. So the judges get into court from just behind the bench. The public, counsel and everyone else involved in a case come into the building via a central hall. They then move outwards, unlike the judges, to get to the individual courtrooms.

The 'new' RCJ, opened by Queen Victoria in 1882, replaced a rabbit warren of slum housing, brothels and taverns. At the grand opening ceremony, the judges presented the Queen with a loyal address. It is said that, when the judges met beforehand to agree on the wording of the loyal address, it was suggested that it should say 'Conscious as we are of our shortcomings', to which one judge objected. He proposed that it should state: 'Conscious as we are of each other's shortcomings . . .'!

Something which particularly helped me in getting to know the RCJ was being appointed to chair a small committee looking at library facilities there for the judges. At that time there was no dedicated judges' library – judges shared a library with litigants-in-person, unrepresented litigants. This was highly unsatisfactory. If a judge went there to consult a book, he or she ran the risk of finding sitting opposite them someone who then appeared in front of them in court – or who had a grievance against the judge because of the outcome of a case. Fortunately a solution was not difficult to find. There existed an attractive Bar Library in the RCJ, which the Bar no longer used very much since the introduction of online law reports and the growth in chambers' own libraries. The Bar had stopped paying for the Bar Library, no doubt because of the underuse. So we recommended that that should become the judges' library, and so it happened.

In the course of our investigations, we were shown by the library staff all the rooms and areas where law books and reports were kept. It was an astonishing collection of spaces. One included part of the roof space at the very top of the building, where several piles of books were scattered about, in some parts getting damp and in others suffering from pigeon droppings. I hope that that no longer persists.

Around this time, I was also able to persuade the Court Service that there was scope to install a gym in the basement of the RCJ. The old boiler room, a huge area originally containing a number of very large old-fashioned boilers, had become available as a result of the installation of modern, efficient and much smaller boilers. I argued that this was a great opportunity to create a gym, which would enable judges and others who worked there to keep fit and healthy, all to the financial benefit of the Court Service. They agreed, it was done, and there is now a well-equipped gym available for – and used by – judges, their clerks, court staff and indeed members of the Bar if their chambers subscribe. It all added to the complex range of facilities in the RCJ, which now include a cafe, a prayer room, a chapel, several libraries, the gym and exhibitions of judicial robes, as well as a strikingly good sculpture of Lord Woolf, the former Lord Chief Justice, made entirely from wire coat hangers!

Towards the end of my time as a High Court judge, I was seconded temporarily to the Court of Appeal to form part of a three-judge court scheduled to hear what was known as the McDonalds libel appeal. This arose out of a cheap, copied leaflet distributed by a number of young environmental activists at suburban railway stations in the London area. It criticized the burger company on a number of grounds, such as the alleged unhealthiness of its food and the way it treated its workforce. Threatened with legal action, most of the activists apologized and withdrew the allegations. Two, however, did not, and McDonalds pursued them to trial for libel.

The two individuals had to represent themselves, because there was no legal aid in libel cases. In contrast, McDonalds retained a leading libel QC, Richard Rampton. The High Court trial lasted the best part of a year and produced generally bad publicity for McDonalds. The two defendants worked assiduously to produce evidence to support their allegations. In the end, the judge found partly in favour of the company, but partly in favour of the activists on the basis that certain of their allegations were true.

Both sides then appealed. We found ourselves having to investigate these allegations ourselves. Were they substantially true or not? It was a long appeal hearing, and in the end we too found certain of the allegations made out. But the appeal process only added to the adverse publicity for McDonalds, and unless one believes that any publicity is to be welcomed, it must have been a commercial own-goal scored by the company. It was, moreover, always going to be extremely expensive for McDonalds, since they had to pay their own legal team and, whatever the outcome, were never going to get any costs or damages from the two individuals.

My time as a High Court Judge lasted six years, because in 2000 I was promoted to the Court of Appeal. That deserves another chapter, before which I shall catch up on more of my family and personal life.

9

France – and the Blairs

*The French are a logical people, which is one reason the
English dislike them so intensely. The other is that they
own France, a country which we have always judged
to be much too good for them.*

ROBERT MORLEY

Like many at the Bar, Gillian and I had wanted some sort of
weekend retreat or holiday home. We had had a small place in
Taunton while I was the candidate there, and later we bought a
cottage in an attractive little village near Shaftesbury called
Berwick St John. It provided us with excellent walking
opportunities in Cranborne Chase, with deciduous woodland
and pheasants thick on the paths. Later in the 1980s we swapped
the cottage for a listed farmhouse in Suffolk close to a village
called Stansfield. The farmhouse had no substantial land but it
did have a duck pond. Eventually we found that the walking in
the vicinity was disappointing. It wasn't just the lack of hills,

which was not as extreme as popular opinion would have it, but the fields were mostly arable and therefore often ploughed, and the farmers tended to plough right to the edge of the field, even cutting up the public footpath. That made for very muddy walking and heavy boots.

Gillian and I both enjoyed hill walking, and over the years we managed to walk a number of long-distance routes. These included the Cotswold Way from Bath to Chipping Campden, the Weald Way from the Thames at Gravesend to the south coast, via the apple orchards of Kent, beautiful in blossom, and the Thames Heritage Way from the Tower of London to Oxford and Blenheim via Hampton Court. Over several years we completed the old pilgrimage route, the Chemin de St Jacques, insofar as it lies in France – from Le Puy in the Massif Central to St Jean Pied de Port by the Spanish border – as well as the Cathar Way, linking most of the ruined Cathar fortresses between Foix and the Mediterranean. That last one we finished in the baking heat of a south-west France summer, ruining my walking boots and exhausting ourselves. Later, we did the Borders Abbeys Way in Scotland and King Ludwig's Way in Bavaria, both with Jill Black and Richard McCombe, judicial colleagues of mine and delightful company. So the absence of good walking in Suffolk was for us a big drawback, even though we should perhaps have anticipated it.

Also the public transport from London to that part of East Anglia was abysmal, meaning that we had to get there by car, which on a Friday late afternoon or evening involved a slow and tiring journey. We began to think about finding instead a place in France, far enough south to ensure sunshine and warmth but within reach of an international airport with flights from the UK. As we did not fancy the Riviera with its congested roads in summer and the large number of Brits, we settled on the area around Toulouse. We knew that that had excellent walking country within easy reach in the shape of the Pyrenees, and Toulouse as the centre of the French aeronautical industry was always likely to have frequent flights to and from the UK.

So we accepted an invitation from a friend, Trevor Phillipson QC, who with his partner Thai Ping Wong owned a chateau in that area near St Gaudens. Our intention was to spend a few days having a look at the area and then go on to Hungary for a holiday. It didn't work out like that. We began house-hunting near the Pyrenees and, though many of the properties we saw were hopeless, we were hooked. Hungary was forgotten and we stayed on. A local estate agent, Gabriel Dubie, eventually told us about a place in a village called St Martin d'Oydes. We were looking for an attractive farmhouse or a *maison du maître*, but this turned out to be a chateau and much bigger than we had envisaged.

But we fell for it. It was built of soft rose-pink brick in about 1500, still had two round towers, a pigeonnier and the remains of a moat, and in the summer sunshine was indescribably romantic. It was built on the site of a twelfth-century stone chateau, some of the remains of which were built into the towers. Inside it turned out to have arrow-slits in the walls, a small oubliette or dungeon in the foot of one of the towers and had once had battlements. Its park contained seven mature cedars and some younger ones, along with some oaks. An attractive hillside rose at the far side of the park. The building had been unoccupied for about eleven years, since the last occupant, a widow, had moved into a care home, leaving the family to argue about its disposal. Before her departure, she and a maid had lived there alone for roughly a decade, ever since her husband had died. It clearly needed a lot of modernizing but seemed solid, and it was on the market for about £150,000.

Would we be welcome in the little village which it adjoined? We asked a small group of locals chatting in the nearby Place du Chateau. 'Mais oui', came the reply, and then in French: 'anyone but Parisians!' (That echoed the comment I had heard a few years before when appearing in south-west Wales for Carmarthen District Council to oppose a Welsh Office road scheme. I apologized to my clients for the situation where they had to use counsel from London. 'Oh no, boyo,' came the response. 'That's fine. Anywhere but Cardiff!' The distrust of those in the rest of the country for the big city and for those from it may perhaps be part of human nature.) Anyway, back to south-west France and to St Martin d'Oydes in particular. The village itself was charming – a complete circle of houses and cottages abutting each other, with just two archways providing access and egress (and they, we discovered, had been a late nineteenth-century innovation). It was a defensive design.

Were we mad to think of buying it? We rang our daughter Harriet, who came over and looked at it and reckoned we were fairly sane. Monsieur Dubie said he had a team of artisans who could put it into good shape for about another £150,000. So we bought it in August 1990. In the end the work needed cost a great deal more than £150,000 and Dubie turned out to be a rogue who failed to pay the members of his *équipe* what we paid him under our contract for the work. There was even litigation in the French courts when some of the artisans sued us for payment, but the courts ruled that our contract was with Dubie, not them, and that we had paid him what was owed. It took several years to get the place rewired, to have running water on the floors above ground level, to put in central heating, to repair the brickwork and so on, but in the end it was done.

The garden completely lacked shrubs and flowers, and planning and planting these gave me an entirely new interest in gardening. We planted some eight magnolias, many roses and clematis, including ones along a newly constructed pergola, and lots of shrubs such as viburnums. I discovered a passion for roses, especially of the climbing variety. There is something very cheering to see in the depths of winter a beautiful white rose like Iceberg climbing high up a wall and still flowering. We knew that we would need a swimming pool for the summer time and found a location where it would not intrude on the views from the chateau.

The pool was only just installed when, in August 1991, we had a phone call from Cherie Blair to say that she and her family were in the area – could they call in? We invited them to lunch, and their kids happily swam in the pool despite the water being a bright green. Cherie, under her maiden name of Cherie Booth, was in the same barristers' chambers as me, which was how she had heard about this chateau we had bought. At this stage our acquaintance with Tony Blair was slight but it grew over the following years, as did their connection with St Martin d'Oydes. Tony at that time was simply the shadow employment minister.

The following summer they came and stayed with us for a few nights at the chateau, and in August 1993 we agreed that they could come for a week. That pattern continued for a few years. By 1993 Tony was now shadow Home Secretary, with John Smith having replaced Neil Kinnock as leader of the Labour Party. The position began to change dramatically in mid-1994, when John Smith suddenly died, and Tony became Leader of the Opposition in October.

The following August (1995) found the Blair family at the chateau again, and this time Tony was preoccupied with preparing his strategy for his speech to the Labour Party conference. His notes read a bit like a shopping list: 'modernize party; modernize country' – but all of it with an emphasis on fairness. He did also find time for a lot of exercise, swimming forty lengths of the pool, playing a lot of tennis and football, and he was clearly physically both strong and fit. We went hill-walking in the lower Pyrenees and visited the ruined Cathar castle at Rocquefixade. On one occasion Peter Goldsmith, who at that time was Chairman of the Bar, came to lunch, with his wife Joy. We decided to have a barbecue lunch outside near the pool, but that required the barbecue to be lit. Tony, Peter and I all struggled to get it to light, and I couldn't avoid wondering what the reaction of the general public would have been if they had been able to observe the difficulty which the Leader of the Opposition, the Chairman of the Bar and a High Court judge were having in grappling with this practical task.

By 1997 the Blair family's visit was a fixture, but things were radically different as a result of Labour's sweeping victory in the May general election. Tony was now Prime Minister, and he and the family came without us but with a Downing Street entourage to stay. There were press photographers climbing up the wall round the perimeter of the garden, French security police in the village and on the hillside behind the house – and much better internet and phone communications! The French dignitaries for the area turned up en masse, from the local mayor to the *préfet*, plus the regional and national representatives. I gather that Tony charmed them all by speaking remarkably fluent French, picked up while working as a youngster in a bar in Paris. More significantly, the French Prime Minister, Lionel Jospin, whose constituency was relatively near, arranged to visit and the two prime ministers met at the chateau.

We overlapped with the Blairs at the chateau in late August 1999, when Tony had evidently been under great strain with the Northern Ireland peace process and with the decision to send troops to Kosovo. He spoke of Gerry Adams saying to him during the Irish discussions: 'The difference is, if it goes wrong for you, you lose an election; if it goes wrong for me, I get shot.' Adams drew a parallel with Michael Collins meeting Lloyd George at No. 10 in 1921 and Collins' assassination the following year. At this point Mo Mowlam pointed to some windows in No. 10 and said: 'It's not that different. Those are the windows broken by the IRA mortar attack in 1991.'

When Tony first came to St Martin d'Oydes as Prime Minster, he played tennis against members of the French security team and beat them. This year the French supplied a member of their police national tennis team and he gave Tony a very hard time. The speed of his serve broke a string on Tony's racket and the player himself was described by Tony as 'bionic' – 'any time I upped my game, he just seemed to turn a switch and stay ahead.'

Tony Blair will, of course, always be remembered for the disastrous invasion of Iraq. That will be seen as his main legacy. In some ways, that is unfortunate, because it masks some other real achievements – the securing of a peaceful settlement in Northern Ireland, the successful intervention in Kosovo, the introduction of a minimum wage, the Human Rights Act and other domestic policy reforms. I suspect that in the long run a more balanced and complex judgment on his tenure of office will prevail.

10

To the Court of Appeal

County lady at dinner party: 'What do you do?'
'I'm a judge.'
'Oh, how splendid! Horses or dogs?'

In early summer of 2000, just before my mother died, I was told
that I was to be promoted to the Court of Appeal. This meant
that I would spend my working days in the Royal Courts of
Justice in London and so that would mean an end to going out
on circuit and presiding over trials. The appointment took effect
at the beginning of October. I became Lord Justice Keene and a
member of the Privy Council, swearing a blood-curdling oath to
inform on any fellow-Privy Counsellor who was plotting against
the Crown – a residue from Tudor times. I got a new clerk, Robin
Cliffe, who was everything that one could wish for – hardworking, very competent, pleasant and unobtrusive. He was also
very experienced in the ways of the Court of Appeal, even down
to the minutiae of the ceremonial dress. That outfit, like the

ceremonial kit of a High Court judge, includes court shoes, so-called, black patent leather but this time with gold buckles instead of silver. How was that to be achieved? The answer was that Robin took away my old court shoes and applied gold paint to the buckles. Lewis Carroll couldn't have improved on it!

It was perhaps inevitable that some parts of the press should run the line, at least by innuendo, that my appointment to the Court of Appeal was the result of my friendship with Tony Blair. That was painful, but only briefly, for I received a very kind note from Tom Bingham, now Lord Bingham of Cornhill and about to conclude a four-year term as Lord Chief Justice, telling me to ignore those press comments and saying that my appointment was the result of a unanimous recommendation by the senior judiciary. It was, he said, done entirely on merit. I was very grateful, especially since this came from him.

Tom Bingham was and is widely regarded by the judiciary as our greatest judge since the Second World War. His career had been astounding: after a first in history at Oxford and a dazzling practice at the Bar, he became a High Court judge at the early age of 46. Six years later he went to the Court of Appeal, of which he became the head as Master of the Rolls in 1992. From there he moved to become Lord Chief Justice, an appointment which initially caused some raised eyebrows at the criminal bar, since he had had only limited experience of criminal work. But he soon demonstrated his mastery of the subject. Finally he became the Senior Law Lord in 2000.

It was, however, his clarity of mind, speed of thought and sense of fairness which impressed one, even more than the formal offices held. On the few occasions on which I sat with him in the Court of Appeal Criminal Division, I observed him producing extempore judgments which were succinct, beautifully expressed and, unlike most extempore judgments, grammatical. He will be remembered for some trenchant comments rejecting the right of the government to detain those suspected of terrorist activity indefinitely without charge, and rejecting the use of evidence which may have been obtained through the use of torture, even if that had taken place not in the UK but in a foreign country. He described reliance upon such evidence as 'unreliable, unfair, offensive to ordinary standards of humanity and decency, and incompatible with the principles which should animate a tribunal seeking to administer justice' (A. *v*. Secretary of State for the Home Department, 2005, para. 52). At all times he sought to uphold the rule of law and the independence of the judiciary.

His sense of fairness permeated his personal as well as his private life. Some years later I invited him to Twickenham to watch the England *v*. France rugby international. He enjoyed the match, but found the partisanship of the crowd disturbing. Rugby spectators do at times shout critical comments when they think the referee has made a bad decision, and this is really just letting off a bit of steam. But Tom couldn't identify with this, such was his innate impartiality.

His comments to me in 2000 on my appointment to the Court of Appeal were greatly appreciated. Nonetheless, I could see that some steps had to be taken to create a distance from Tony Blair, especially as much of my work in the Court of Appeal was likely to involve judicial review cases brought by the citizen against a public body, often a government department. There was a risk that, sooner or later, counsel for a litigant in such a case was going to object to my hearing it. So that August 2000 was the last time that the Blair family came to the chateau. I explained the problem to Tony, who immediately understood and agreed that they would go elsewhere.

I found the work in the Court of Appeal very satisfying. Even though it is not the final court of appeal in the land, the number of cases which go on to that final court – the House of Lords judicial committee pre-2009, the Supreme Court from 2009 – are relatively few. So most cases involving a point of law stop at the Court of Appeal. Thus one has the opportunity to interpret the law and, in reality, to make law to a certain extent. Of course, one sits with two other judges in the Court of Appeal and it is sometimes a challenge to persuade the other two of a particular point. Sometimes one is persuaded out of one's own initial view. And sometimes one ends up in a minority, writing a dissenting judgment. The implementation of the Human Rights Act 1998 as from October 2000 made this a particularly interesting time, especially with the development of a right to privacy. Such a right needs, of course, always to be balanced against freedom of expression and the freedom of the press, but I was always firmly of the view that a person's private life was not to be given publicity unless either the public interest justified it or the person had in some way acted so as to invite such publicity. Nor does 'public interest' arise merely because the public would find the disclosures interesting or entertaining. That would justify quite extreme intrusions into private life.

It is inevitable that, when you have a court of three judges, not all of them will be specialists in the particular area of law involved in the case to be heard. In most instances there will be one judge who does have such specialist knowledge, occasionally even two, but the others will not. I found that there was considerable value in having one or two non-specialists in the composition of the court. He or she can ask the very basic questions during argument without any sense of embarrassment, since counsel in the case will be well aware that this judge is not a specialist. Moreover, such a mix of judges allows for some cross-fertilization from other branches of the law, perhaps bringing for example some principles of judicial review to bear on a tax case. The only problem arises if you have two specialists amongst the three and the two then disagree! It is left to the non-specialist to decide which is right. Not necessarily a bad thing but quite demanding.

One dramatic event in the summer of 2003 remains vivid in my memory. I had recently become Chairman of the Judicial Studies Board, the body responsible for the training of judges and magistrates in England and Wales (now known as the Judicial College). In that capacity I was invited to join a small group of senior judges for an away-day at Minster Lovell in Oxfordshire to discuss current issues. Into a mini bus at the Royal Courts of Justice piled Harry Woolf (Lord Woolf of Barnes, the Lord Chief Justice), Elizabeth Butler-Sloss, Head of the Family Division, the other Heads of Division, some other senior judges and me. It was clear that Harry knew that something was about to happen, because he got the driver to keep the radio on, tuned to a news channel. Sure enough, as we drove through West London and beyond, we heard the announcement that the Lord Chancellor's post was being abolished, Derry Irvine sacked and a whole range of constitutional changes being implemented, including the creation of a Supreme Court. Eventually, the government found that abolishing the position of Lord Chancellor was impractical and it was retained, but with the occupant no longer head of the judiciary. The other changes eventually found expression in the Constitutional Reform Act 2005. But the confusion over the position of Lord Chancellor, plus Harry Woolf's reaction, made it evident that neither he nor the senior judiciary had been consulted. It was not a sensible way to carry out major reform to the constitution. The announcements dominated the work of our away-day, with Harry regularly being called away to take phone calls from Charlie Falconer, the new Secretary of State for Constitutional Affairs.

In the period between that announcement of June 2003 and the passing of the Constitutional Reform Act in 2005, there was much debate about the shape of the new arrangements. At one stage it was proposed that the new body for judicial appointments should, in the case of senior positions such as the Lord Chief Justice, send two names to the Prime Minister, who would then choose between them. I remonstrated with Charlie Falconer on one occasion, arguing that it would be wrong to have such political involvement in the appointment of very senior judges. He sought to defend it, saying that the Lord Chief Justice needed to be somebody who could get on with the government and vice versa. I disagreed and pointed out that someone who was chosen by the Prime Minister from one party might well be anathema to the government if and when power changed hands at a general election. Eventually, that proposal was dropped.

It is a relatively new principle in our constitution that the judiciary and the government should be and should be seen to be quite separate from each other. Only about a hundred years ago it was thought to be routine for the Attorney-General of the day, normally a political animal, to be offered the post of Lord Chief Justice when that fell vacant. One striking example concerns Sir Rufus Isaacs, later the Marquess of Reading. In 1913 he was the Attorney-General and actually was a member of the Liberal Cabinet under Asquith. The position of Lord Chief Justice fell vacant and Isaacs sought and obtained the position. No-one seems to have thought that move from government to Lord Chief Justice at all extraordinary. Things have changed completely since then, partly because the growth of judicial review has meant that the courts now deal with many cases in which a government department is one of the parties.

The job of Chairman of the Judicial Studies Board was very much an extra, to be fitted in on top of normal Court of Appeal duties. I regarded the training of judges, both on their appointment and while in post, as very necessary. That had not always been a widespread view. I was told that initially, when a training body was proposed in 1979, it was to be called the Judicial Training Board. However, some judges objected, on the basis that they did not need training. So it was camouflaged as the Judicial Studies Board. By the time I took over in 2003 there was universal acceptance amongst the judiciary that training was at least highly desirable. I had certainly found it so, coming to criminal cases with virtually no experience as a barrister of such work. The JSB ran courses, some one-day, some over weekends, with mock trials often featuring in the longer sessions. It produced loose-leaf books, 'bench books', for the assistance of judges on a range of subjects, and it held the occasional evening lecture. The fundamental principle was, and I believe still is, that judges should be in charge of training judges – not the Court Service, not civil servants, but judges. Only that way can the independence of the judiciary be ensured.

Too much of the Court of Appeal's work consisted of immigration cases, but we did also cover the full range of civil and criminal litigation. I found sitting on criminal appeals, where as the Lord Justice I had to preside, very satisfying. Sometimes they revealed convictions which had been obtained in troubling circumstances. In one case, a man had been convicted of murder largely because metal filings had been found both in his car and on the dress of the victim. These tiny filings had been described at trial by an expert witness for the prosecution as of a very rare composition. The evidence placed before us in the Court of Appeal Criminal Division was that they were anything but rare. They were the typical particles of metal that flew off a cheap cigarette lighter when it was flicked. We quashed the conviction. A few years later I was informed that another man had been convicted of that murder. The case underlines the fact that the administration of justice is fallible. Juries and judges are human and sometimes make mistakes. That has confirmed me in the view that it would be utterly wrong to bring back the death penalty for murder. Ever since university I have considered that that sentence was unjustified morally or practically, but I now see that it would also be unacceptable because of its finality. It is regrettable enough when a wrongly convicted person spends years in jail before his innocence is revealed, but at least he can then be released. The death penalty allows no such mitigation.

I sat in family law cases and intellectual property cases, though always with at least one colleague who was more of a specialist in the field. It made for a stimulating mix. It was enlivened still more for me by my appointment as the Chairman of the body seeking to advance contacts with the French judiciary. I took this over from Nicholas Phillips (Lord Phillips of Worth Matravers). One of its characteristics was that it was the Franco-*British* Committee, so that it also involved on our side of the Channel judges from Scotland and Northern Ireland. It led to me meeting Robert Reed (now Lord Reed), a Scottish judge, and renewing contact with Brian Kerr (Lord Kerr of Tonaghmore) from Northern Ireland, both of whom have remained good friends, but I have always found it regrettable that there is not a body which brings together judges from the whole of the United Kingdom. Why should we have to have French judges as a cover?

One discovery I made in the discussions with French judges was that, though they would tackle a particular case from a very different starting point from that used by an English judge, we generally ended up with the same answer. They would begin with the provisions of their Code, stemming originally from the days of Napoleon, while we would often be seeking to apply the common law, the principles derived from past decisions by judges in cases over many years. Yet as each side took on board the facts of the individual case and its merits, we found ourselves moving closer together. I found that encouraging. It seemed to demonstrate that, as far as possible, litigation in the courts should produce a result that was sensible and fair.

The meetings with our French colleagues always tested my command of the French language, sometimes beyond breaking point. My linguistic ability can readily be seen from an episode when Gillian and I were on holiday in south-west France and called at a vineyard. We pulled up in our hire car, I got out and a man appeared from a barn. 'Bonjour,' I said. 'Ah,' he replied, 'wait a moment. I will get my wife. She speaks better English than I do'! Still, the Franco-British connection led to one further Prime Ministerial meeting: Nicholas Phillips and I went to Paris to plan one of the conferences and he arranged for us to stay in the British Embassy, a beautiful building of the eighteenth century, once owned by Napoleon's sister who sold it to the Duke of Wellington. There in the garden we came across John Major, now retired as Prime Minister, with his secretary, about to launch his memoirs in France. He seemed to me to be a man of great charm and impressive ability.

One problem we didn't train judges to deal with was that of keeping awake on the bench! That was not normally difficult, but on warm summer afternoons after lunch there has been the odd incident, especially if the advocate addressing the court is unexciting in tone. I came across this problem on one occasion in the Court of Appeal, in just such circumstance, where I noticed that one of our number was finding it difficult to remain alert. The judge's head would start to drop, and then would jerk back up when realisation of what was happening broke through. Fortunately, I had been prepared years before for dealing with such a situation. As a new High Court judge, I asked a more experienced colleague how to ensure that one stayed awake in the most adverse conditions. 'Smelling salts,' he advised. 'What?' I replied. 'I thought those went out in Victorian times.' 'No,' came his response, 'just go down to Boots and you will find them there.' I did and they were there. Thereafter I kept the little pot of smelling salts, with their aroma of ammonia, in the pocket of my judge's robes. I rarely had to use them, but on this summer's afternoon in the Court of Appeal they came into their own. I passed the pot discreetly along the bench to my colleague, who took it unobtrusively and apparently without surprise, recognizing it for what it was. It was used equally discreetly and was eventually returned to me.

Although work in the Court of Appeal was demanding, I had little hesitation during my time there in accepting a suggestion that I might serve as Treasurer of the Inner Temple, my Inn of Court. I had been a bencher of the Inn for some years and had found that getting involved in the affairs of the Inn was very satisfying. I made many new friends. I served on the Estates Committee and the Library Committee, and then in 2006 I became Treasurer, the most senior position in the Inn, one which is held just for the calendar year. It meant that I discovered in much more detail how the Inn was run, how dedicated its staff were and how very supportive they were to the Treasurer. It also involved me in making a considerable number of after-dinner speeches. That I enjoyed. Most judges, having originally been advocates, enjoy the chance to indulge in a bit of public speaking again, and I gradually learned some techniques – not to rush, but to take time, to seem confident and, after telling a joke, to pause for the hoped-for laughter. I began to recall Harold Macmillan's skill in such performances and wished that I could approach anywhere near his level of achievement.

Meanwhile our family had been increasing in number. Ned and Molly were in Oxford when their first daughter, Olivia, was born – our first grandchild was the occasion for great celebration. She soon displayed a mind of her own and, even before she could speak, was seen to roll her eyes at the perceived stupidity of her father. She was followed two years later by Rosalind (Rosie), who was born in the USA, as Ned and Molly were then working at Georgia Tech in Atlanta. Rosalind at birth was a tall, heavy baby, in contrast to the slender graceful ballerina she became. Then came Lily in 2007, full of character and a real performer. Harriet had not found anyone she wanted to settle down with permanently, but wanted to have children, so she opted for single motherhood. This courageous decision she carried out by IVF using a donor, and the result was first Violet and then two years later Florence, full sisters since the donor was the same. Both are very intelligent and independent-minded.

Harriet and her two daughters lived in London, while Ned and Molly came back to Oxford, where they both got university teaching jobs, Ned at Christ Church and Molly at Oxford Brookes. Gillian and I began to think about our own domestic arrangements. We had been living in Belsize Park for nearly thirty years, and our house had increased hugely in value. Both our children would benefit if we released some capital, and I also knew that I would have no difficulty in getting a rented flat in the Inner Temple, were we to move out of London. So that is what we did. In 2005 we sold our Belsize Lane house and bought one in north Oxford.

Oxford had always had an attraction for us, in part as the place where we had first met and where our lives had radically changed. We knew that we had friends there, as well as there being many other interesting people. It was full of beautiful buildings, had a compact central area and was within an hour's train journey of London. That mattered – I was still working in London and we had many friends and much social life there. Balliol, to my surprise and great delight, had made me an Honorary Fellow in 2004, which strengthened my feelings of affection for the place. I had never imagined as a callow and nervous undergraduate that one day I might find myself being welcomed into the Senior Common Room. Gillian had been involved for some time with the Family Welfare Association, and in due course, when the FWA amalgamated with another body working in the same field, the combined organization became known as Family Action. Gillian became its Chairman for a number of years.

The house which she found in north Oxford was very conveniently located, not merely in terms of access to the city centre but also because it was located between the senior and junior parts of the Oxford High School for Girls, where all three of Ned and Molly's girls came to be educated. In due course that meant, as it still does, that we often enjoyed them calling in on us after school was over for the day.

The flat in the Inner Temple was, like all the premises in the Inn, rented. It has a delightful view from the main rooms looking eastwards, across the Inn's gardens towards the dome of St Paul's. It is on the fourth floor, but unlike many of the flats in the Temple, it has the benefit of a lift. It has also enabled me in later years, when retired, to keep up my contacts with friends and colleagues in the Inn.

11

The Home Straight

But though an old man, I am but a young gardener.
THOMAS JEFFERSON

By early 2009, I had served almost fifteen years as a full-time judge – six in the High Court and nearly nine in the Court of Appeal – and I was therefore on the verge of qualifying for the full judicial pension. I did not need to retire, in that I was just approaching my 68th birthday and would not hit the age limit until I reached 75. However, I was very conscious of two things: first, that there were many other aspects of life apart from the law, places to travel to, theatres and cinemas to visit, grandchildren's company to enjoy; and secondly, the duration of one's remaining years was highly uncertain. The unpredictability of that had been brought home to me by the deaths of friends and relatives – Phillip Whitehead, a good friend from Oxford days, suddenly dropped dead of a heart attack on New Year's Eve

2005; Alan Coren went almost as suddenly in 2007; and then the following year, Gillian's younger sister, Katharine, only 57, also died. It seemed to underline the relevance of that piece of verse 'Don't ask the Gods how long you've got, For they may answer "Not a Lot"'. Anyway, I took the decision to retire as from October 2009 and duly informed the head of the Court of Appeal.

I wasn't proposing to stop working completely. That, I reckoned, would be a mistake. I continued to sit from time to time as an additional judge in the Court of Appeal, one of those retired Lord Justices of Appeal known to their colleagues as 'retreads' or 'returned empties'! It had the great advantage that I could more or less choose how often I sat and so how much work I did. I carried on like that until 2016, when I reached the mandatory retirement age. I was one of the fortunate generation of judges when it came to judicial retirement pensions. One of the attractions of a place on the bench when I was appointed was the judicial pension, up to half final salary depending on how many years' service had passed. It made up to some extent for the large drop in income that usually accompanied the move from the bar to the bench. In my case, my income dropped to about one-third of what it had been, and that was true of many others appointed. But the pension, a desire to make decisions in cases and often a sense of public duty made up for it. Recent changes, however, in the pension arrangements affecting those appointed to the bench in the last few years have in many cases robbed the judicial pension of much or all of its value. If the person in question has saved for a private pension while at the bar, this can now reduce his or her judicial pension to zero. Unsurprisingly this had had a serious adverse effect on recruitment to the bench. It is now increasingly difficult to get the most able barristers to become judges. On one recent round of selection, the Judicial Appointments Commission found itself having to leave a number of High Court positions unfilled because candidates of sufficient quality had not applied. One can only admire the Commission's courage in choosing not to water down the quality of the High Court bench, but what a sad state of affairs! One can only hope that the Secretary of State for Justice will realize the need to act before it is too late.

In my own retirement, not only did I have my pension, but other opportunities also appeared. I decided to qualify as an arbitrator and I then became a 'door tenant' (practising from a set of chambers without working from their premises), first of my old chambers at 4 and 5 Gray's Inn Square, and then at 39 Essex Street, now known as 39 Essex Chambers, which had more arbitration work. My work as an arbitrator was fairly slow to develop, no doubt because I was not known as a commercial law specialist, but I tended to get cases where technical issues like engineering arose. I found myself dealing with cases involving North Sea oil rigs. In addition, I was asked by Harry Woolf if I would become a judge of a new international court over which he was presiding in Qatar. I agreed and in due course became the Deputy President, before moving sideways to become the Chairman of the court's junior branch, a Tribunal which heard appeals from decisions of the regulatory bodies in Qatar. Again, the work was limited in volume, but that suited me.

That was especially the case because I had been persuaded to become a member of the selection panel which chose new Queen's Counsel. Its procedures were sometimes criticized as bureaucratic, but that was probably inevitable, because the Panel had no information, no historic files about the applicants, other than the material put before it by those applicants and their referees. What came as a surprise was the substantial burden of work involved during the summer holiday season. I managed two years on the panel and then, like my judicial predecessor and successor, I decided that I had done my duty.

More interesting was becoming involved with the Slynn Foundation, of which I became a trustee. The Foundation sought to assist the judiciary in various parts of the world, initially the former Communist bloc states, to become both truly independent of government and more efficient. To this end I and other retired judges, and sometimes barristers and ex-civil servants, visited those countries, though only if our help was sought. I found myself in Albania and Serbia, and later in the Middle East. Gillian came with me to Egypt in what proved to be a very small window of opportunity after the Arab Spring, when conditions were fairly relaxed and peaceful. Much to our pleasure we were invited to stay with the British Ambassador in the Residence in Cairo, a building still redolent of Curzon and boasting the first sprung ballroom in Africa! Its garden originally extended down to the banks of the Nile, but sadly had since been separated from the river by a major road. The by-product of that trip was the discovery of live cinema broadcasts from the New York Metropolitan Opera, to one of which James Watt, the Ambassador, invited us. Gillian and I had long been fans of opera (other than Wagner), so this was a very welcome find. We have an excellent cinema in Oxford which shows a lot of live opera and plays, not only from the Met, but also from Covent Garden and the National Theatre.

My knowledge and appreciation of classical music lagged far behind my experience of opera, but moving to Oxford led to my recruitment as a trustee of the Oxford Philomusica, now known as the Oxford Philharmonic. This was the brainchild of Marios Papadopoulos, who along with his wife Anthi raised funds for the orchestra, organized concerts, and engaged distinguished soloists. Marios also conducted and played the piano. The concerts introduced us, late in life, to a much wider range of classical music. I also greatly enjoy being a member of the Garrick club, a relaxed and hospitable place, largely frequented by lawyers and actors.

There is now little more to record. We enjoy the benefit of a large circle of good friends, including by some coincidence a number of retired GPs and medical specialists – always useful at this time of life! Some of them are involved, as I am, in an Oxford-based walking group which was started by Sir Roger Bannister of four-minute mile fame. We meet once a month and walk for the morning and then have a pub lunch. Sadly, Roger could no longer manage the walks by the time I joined because of increasing disability, but he usually managed to join us for the lunch. He told me once how he recently had been addressing a group of schoolchildren and, when it was over, one small girl came up to him and said: 'Are you really Roger Bannister?' He replied 'yes'. 'Really, the Roger Bannister?' 'Yes'. 'We've just done you in history!'

We are about to put the chateau in France onto the market so as to simplify our lives, a very sad step after putting much time, money and effort into it over twenty-eight years. We shall be sorry to leave, but as Gillian and I both grow older, it makes sense to simplify our lives. We shall miss the friends that we have made in that lovely part of France, but fortunately it seems that some of them may welcome us back to stay with them for a while. Chris and Malcolm Grant, she a recently retired GP, he the former Provost of University College London, liked the area so much when they were staying with us that they bought a house less than half an hour's drive away, with beautiful views of the Pyrenees. They have always been very hospitable and we have high hopes that they might occasionally welcome us back.

I am still doing some legal work, and I have just finished another international arbitration this spring. But above all, I have been blessed with a wonderful family, to whom I hope these few words will be of some interest. I also hope to survive for a few more years to see what my granddaughters achieve. One has to try to be philosophical about ageing. When we went to visit Troy a few years ago, I read the *Iliad*, something which (to my shame) I had never done before, and I was struck by one passage, with which I will end:

> Men in their generations are like the leaves of the trees. The wind blows and one year's leaves are scattered on the ground; but the trees burst into bud and put on fresh ones when the spring comes round. In the same way one generation flourishes and another nears its end.
>
> The Iliad, book VI

Appendix

Short Biographical Notes

Sir **Roger Bannister** CH, CBE: a distinguished neurologist and athlete. The first person to run a mile in under four minutes, which he did in 1954. Later, Master of Pembroke College, Oxford. Died March 2018.

Sir **Christopher Bellamy** QC: a judge of the Court of First Instance of the European Communities, 1992–99. Chairman of the Competition Appeal Tribunal 1997–2007.

Lord Bingham of Cornhill KG, PC, formerly Sir Thomas Bingham: outstanding judge. In turn, Master of the Rolls, Lord Chief Justice and Senior Law Lord. Helped to bring about the creation of the UK Supreme Court. Author of *The Rule of Law*. Earlier, scholar of Balliol College, Oxford, where he was President of the JCR, and Eldon Scholar. Died 2010.

Tony Blair: UK Prime Minister 1997–2007. Previously held various shadow cabinet posts, and was Leader of the Opposition 1994–97. Married to Cherie Blair, née Booth. Introduced minimum wage and negotiated Good Friday Agreement in Northern Ireland. Took part in US-led invasion of Iraq in 2003.

Professor Sir **Colin Buchanan** CBE: town planner and author of *Traffic in Towns* (1963). Member of the Roskill Commission on the Third London Airport. President both of the Royal Town Planning Institute and the Council for the Protection of Rural England. Died 2001.

William ('Bill') Coolidge: American lawyer and financier. Read PPE at Balliol College, Oxford, of which he was a benefactor and an Honorary Fellow. Started the Pathfinder awards at Balliol. Died 1992.

Alan Coren: humorous writer and Editor of *Punch*. Performed in 'The News Quiz' and 'Call My Bluff'. Author of *Golfing For Cats, The Sanity Inspector, 69 for 1* and many other books, including the Arthur series for children. Married to Anne, a consultant anaesthetist, and father of Giles Coren and Victoria Coren Mitchell. The funniest English writer of his time. Died 2007.

Lord Denning OM, PC, formerly Sir Alfred ('Tom') Denning: Master of the Rolls and Law Lord. A judge for thirty-eight years, including twenty years as head of the Court of Appeal. Wrote the colourful report into the Profumo affair, 1963. An innovative judge and lawyer. Former Eldon Scholar. Died 1999, aged 100.

George Dobry CBE, QC: distinguished and entertaining planning barrister, educated at Warsaw University. Founder of British-Polish Legal Association and a founder of the Slynn Foundation. Author of many books on legal topics, especially planning, and sometime adviser to government on planning law. Became a circuit judge 1980. Died March 2018.

Professor **Rigas Doganis**: leading airline economist and author of several books on that subject. Was Chairman and CEO of Olympic Airways and later a non-executive director of Easyjet. Professor of Air Transport at Cranfield University in the 1990s. Educated at Hampton Grammar School and LSE.

Sir **Edward du Cann** KBE, PC: Conservative MP for Taunton from 1956 to 1987 and party Chairman from 1965 to 1967. Had a chequered career as a company director, several of his companies going bankrupt, and his property being repossessed. Retired to live in Cyprus. Died 2017.

Sir **Graham Eyre** QC: one of the most outstanding planning barristers and QCs of his generation. A brilliant advocate whose cross-examination of expert witnesses was devastating. Acted as the inspector at the Stansted/Heathrow public inquiry 1981–83. Died aged only 68 in 1999.

Lord Falconer PC, QC, formerly Charles ('Charlie') Leslie Falconer: successful commercial barrister and friend of Tony Blair. Became a peer in 1997 and Solicitor-General in Blair's first term as Prime Minister and subsequently Lord Chancellor and Secretary of State for Constitutional Affairs. Introduced the Freedom of Information Act, providing for public access to information held by public authorities.

Sir **Douglas Frank** QC: stylish planning barrister who built up chambers at 4 and 5 Gray's Inn Square into a leading set. Became President of the Lands Tribunal, dealing with issues about valuation of land. Died 2004.

Hugh Gaitskell CBE, MP: Leader of the Labour Party 1955–63 and, as such, Leader of the Opposition. An economist and civil servant before becoming an MP, he held various posts in Clement Attlee's government, eventually becoming the Chancellor of the Exchequer for one year from October 1950.

Lord Justice Henry PC, formerly Sir Denis Henry: barrister, QC and later judge, first of the High Court and then of the Court of Appeal. Presided over the Guinness shareholding fraud trials. Chairman of the Judicial Studies Board 1994–99. Educated at

Shrewsbury School and Balliol College, Oxford, where he obtained a half-blue at golf. Died in 2010.

Lord Irvine of Lairg PC, QC, formerly Alexander Andrew Mackay Irvine and known as 'Derry' Irvine: barrister and a legal adviser to the Labour Party in the 1980s. Pupil-master to Tony Blair and Cherie Booth. Shadow Lord Chancellor under John Smith's leadership of the Labour Party and then Lord Chancellor in the Blair government from 1997 to 2003. Pioneered the introduction of the Human Rights Act 1998, which incorporated the European Convention on Human Rights into United Kingdom law.

Nicholas de B. Katzenbach: American lawyer and Deputy Attorney-General of the USA from 1962 to 1965 under Presidents Kennedy and Johnson. Became Attorney-General in 1965, shortly after Bobby Kennedy quit the post in order to run for the US Senate from New York. Educated Yale Law School and Balliol College, Oxford, where he was a Rhodes Scholar. Died 2012.

John Fitzgerald Kennedy: 35th President of the USA and the youngest to hold that office, aged 43. Successfully handled the Cuba missile crisis. Assassinated in November 1963 after less than three years in office.

Mark Littman QC: one of the most successful commercial law silks of his day. Tall and charming, he was Treasurer of the Middle Temple in 1988. Died 2015, aged 94.

Lord Mackay of Clashfern PC, QC, formerly James Mackay: Scottish advocate. The son of a railway signalman, he became Lord Advocate in Scotland in 1979. He was Lord Chancellor under Margaret Thatcher and John Major for almost ten years, far longer than any of his successors. An unassuming man wholly lacking in pomposity, he was raised a member of the Free Presbyterian Church of Scotland but in effect expelled for attending funeral masses of judicial colleagues who had been Catholics.

Harold Macmillan, Earl of Stockton, OM, PC: a 'One Nation' Conservative. Influenced by memories of the Depression, he held several high offices in government under Sir Anthony Eden. On the latter's resignation in 1957, Macmillan became Prime Minister, a position he held until 1963. Nicknamed 'Supermac' by the press, he will be remembered amongst other things for his 'Wind of Change' speech to the South African Parliament and for his support for the independence of Britain's colonial possessions in Africa. Educated at Eton and Balliol College, Oxford. Died in 1986 aged 92.

Sir **Konrad Schiemann** PC, QC: barrister and eventually judge. Orphaned in Germany during the Second World War, he came to England in 1946. Practised mainly as a planning barrister at 4 and 5 Gray's Inn Square, before becoming a High Court judge in 1986 and a Lord Justice of Appeal in 1995. Between 2004 and

2012 he was a judge of the European Court of Justice in Luxembourg.

Lord Taylor of Gosforth PC: Peter Taylor grew up in the northeast of England, where in due course he practised as a barrister, concentrating on criminal cases. He prosecuted in many well-known trials, including that of Jeremy Thorpe, the former Liberal Party leader, for murder. He was made a High Court judge in 1980, a member of the Court of Appeal eight years later and Lord Chief Justice in 1992. Before that, he had conducted an inquiry into the Hillsborough football stadium disaster. He was a talented pianist, who could be seen (and heard) practising at lunchtime in the Inner Temple from time to time. His tenure of the post of Lord Chief Justice was cut tragically short by the development of a brain tumour. He died, aged only 66, in 1997.

Phillip Whitehead MP and MEP: a television documentary producer and politician, he was in his time at Oxford University a Conservative where he was both President of the Union and President of the University Conservative Association. Having seen the light after leaving Oxford, he changed parties and became Labour MP for Derby North in 1970. He continued as such for the next thirteen years. Later he became a member of the European Parliament, a position he held until his death. He was a prolific writer on political topics. Known to some of his friends as 'Fidel', because of the similarity of his beard to that of

Castro, he died suddenly from a heart attack on New Year's Eve 2005, aged 68.

Lord Woolf of Barnes CH, PC: Harry Woolf was a barrister and judge, the latter role being one he still performs overseas since his retirement. He was, as Master of the Rolls, head of the civil section of the Court of Appeal before becoming Lord Chief Justice in 2000. Earlier, his report on the riots at Strangeways Prison and elsewhere was highly critical of the conditions within the prisons. On retirement from the bench in 2005, he carried on an active professional life: he was the first President of a new international court in Qatar, and he chairs the Council of University College London. He is currently establishing a new international court in Kazakhstan.

Richard Yorke QC: colourful and generous barrister, practising mainly in commercial law. An enthusiastic sailor and small aircraft pilot. A graduate of Balliol College, Oxford. Died 1991 after suffering a brain tumour.

INDEX